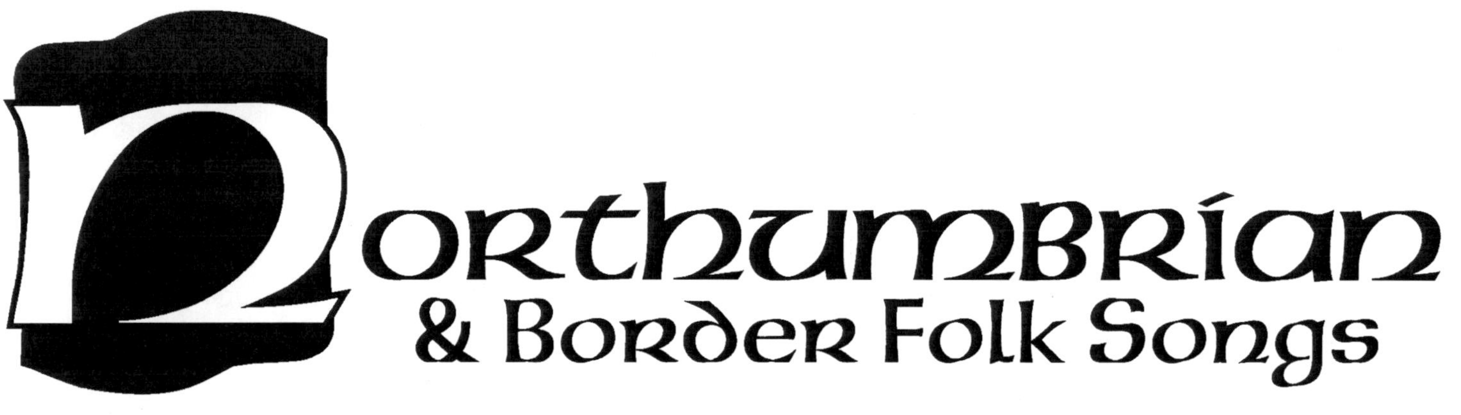

# Northumbrian & Border Folk Songs

## Melodies for Fingerstyle Guitar

by Bill Brennan

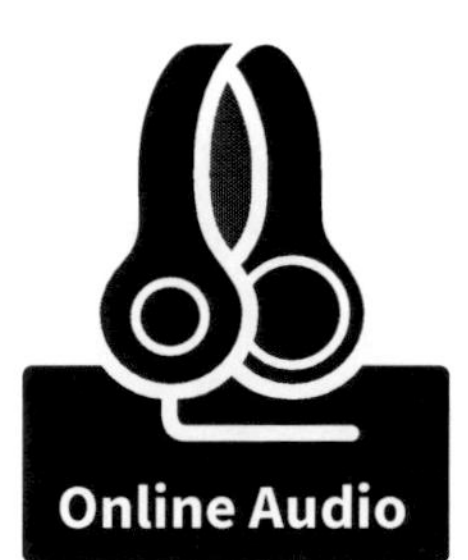


www.melbay.com/96475BCDEB

**AUDIO CONTENTS**

| | | | |
|---|---|---|---|
| 1 | My Love is Newly Listed | 11 | Sweet Hesleyside |
| 2 | Salmon Tails Up the Water | 12 | Chevy Chase |
| 3 | Hesleyside Reel | 13 | Lea Riggs |
| 4 | Johnny Armstrong | 14 | Noble Squire Dacre |
| 5 | Jimmy Allen | 15 | Dolia |
| 6 | Felton Lonnen | 16 | Are You My Hinny Burd |
| 7 | Sir John Fenwick | 17 | The Breamish |
| 8 | A Bonny Gallowgate Lad | 18 | Blow the Wind Southerly |
| 9 | Buy Broom Besoms | 19 | Here's the Tender Coming |
| 10 | Elsie Marley | 20 | Waters of Tyne |

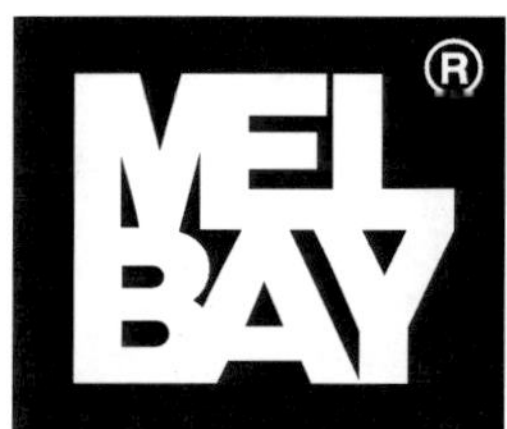




***Visit us on the Web at www.melbay.com — E-mail us at email@melbay.com***

# Acknowledgments

I would like to thank the following people for their valuable help with this book:
Yvonne Brennan, Beth Brennan, Tommy Doyle, Eric Robertson, Brian Watson.

# Contents

# My Love is Newly Listed
## (The Snows)

Thomas Doubleday, a 19th century music publisher and collector of Northumbrian music, picked this tune up from a street singer shortly before 1821. He gave it some verses and called the song "The Snow it Melts the Soonest," and this is the name it is commonly called today.

Technical Notes - Tune the guitar DADGAD, low to high. Although in 12/8 time this tune should be played in a pretty loose style.

Let bass notes sustain as this gives a pretty good imitation of the bagpipe drones.

In the second last bar keep the left hand fingers on the fretted notes as long as possible in order that the notes ring on.

# My Love is Newly Listed
## (The Snows)

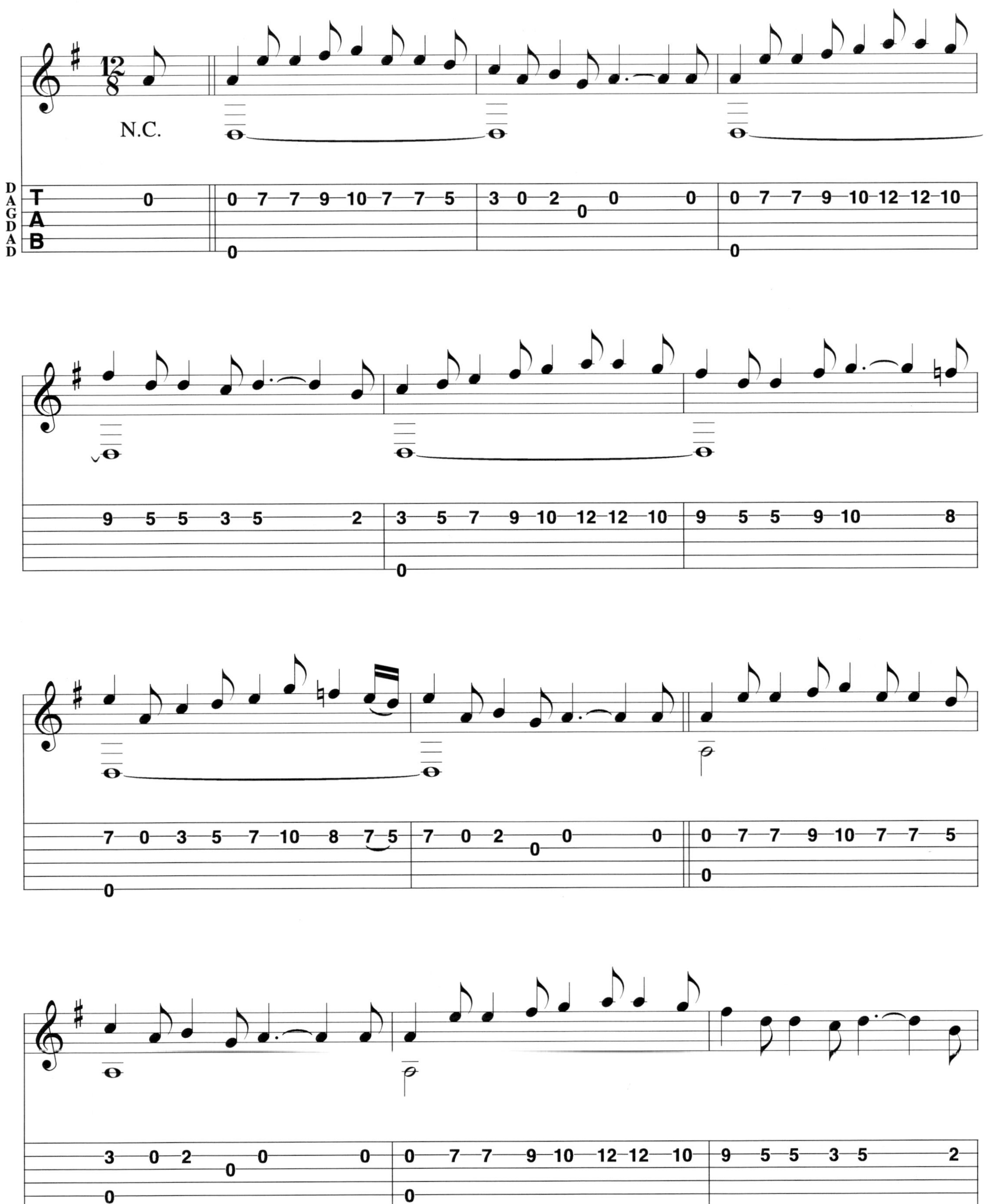

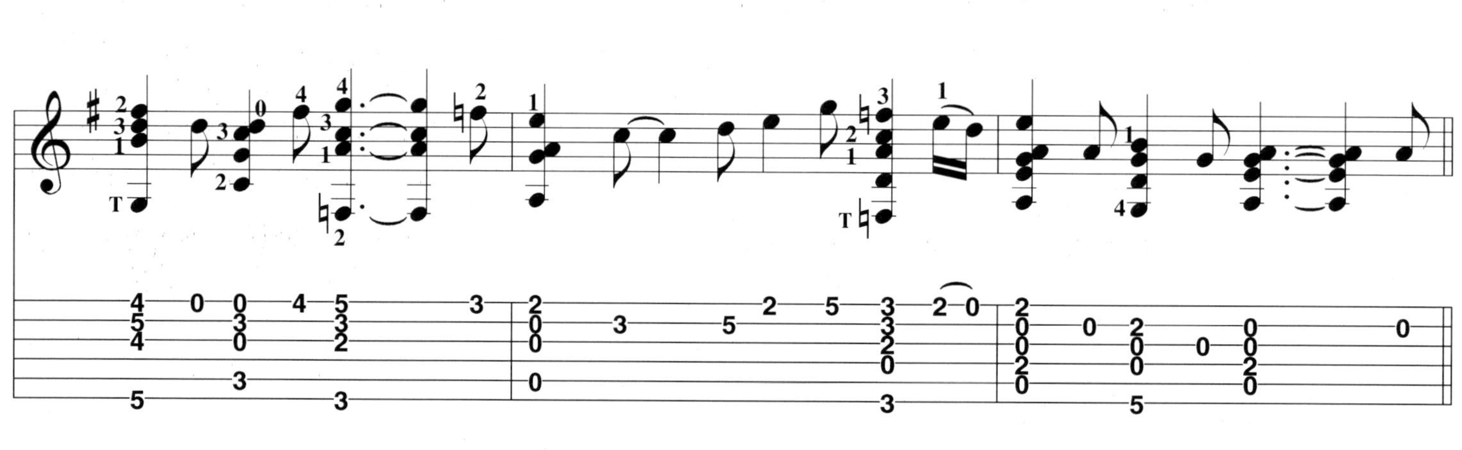

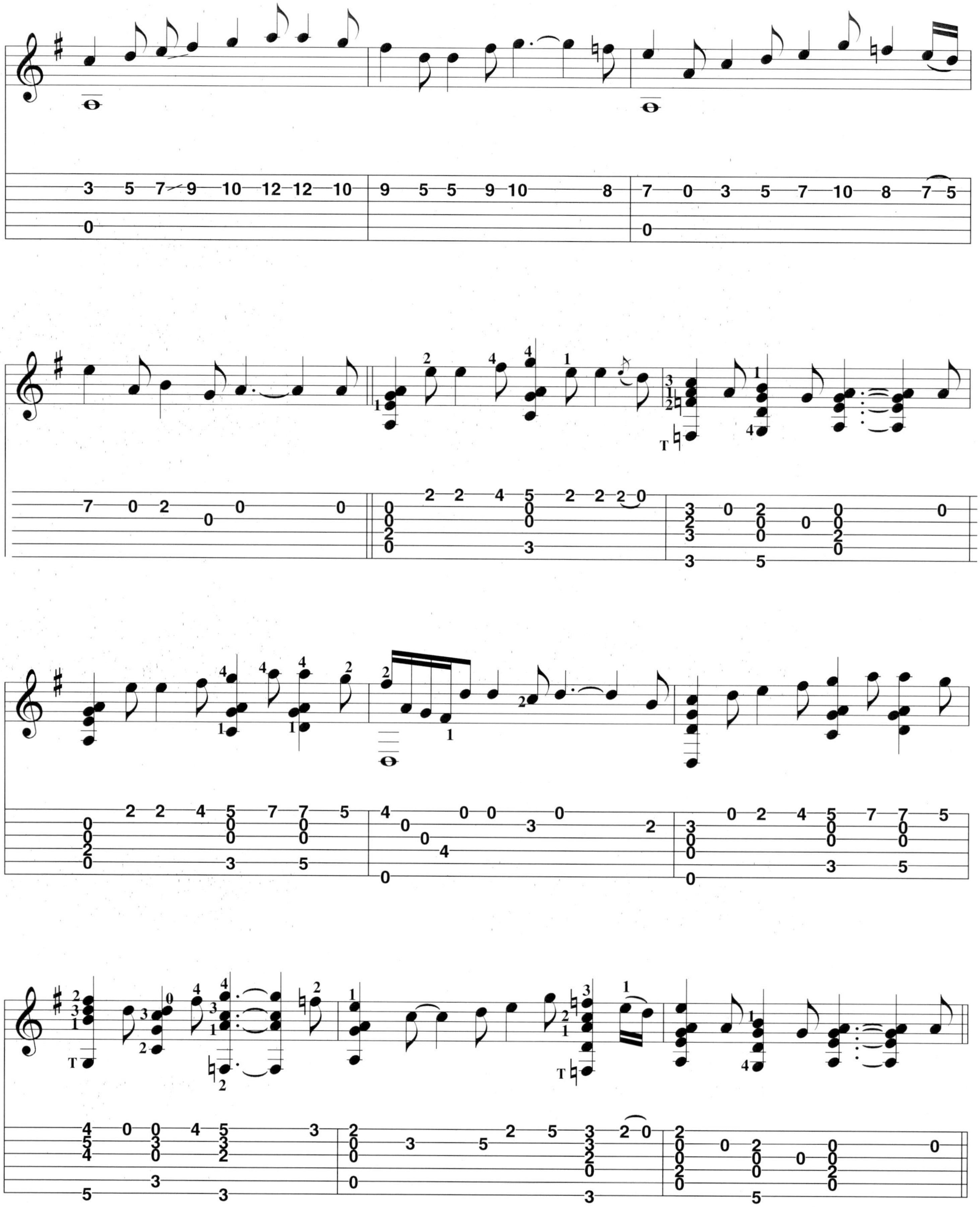

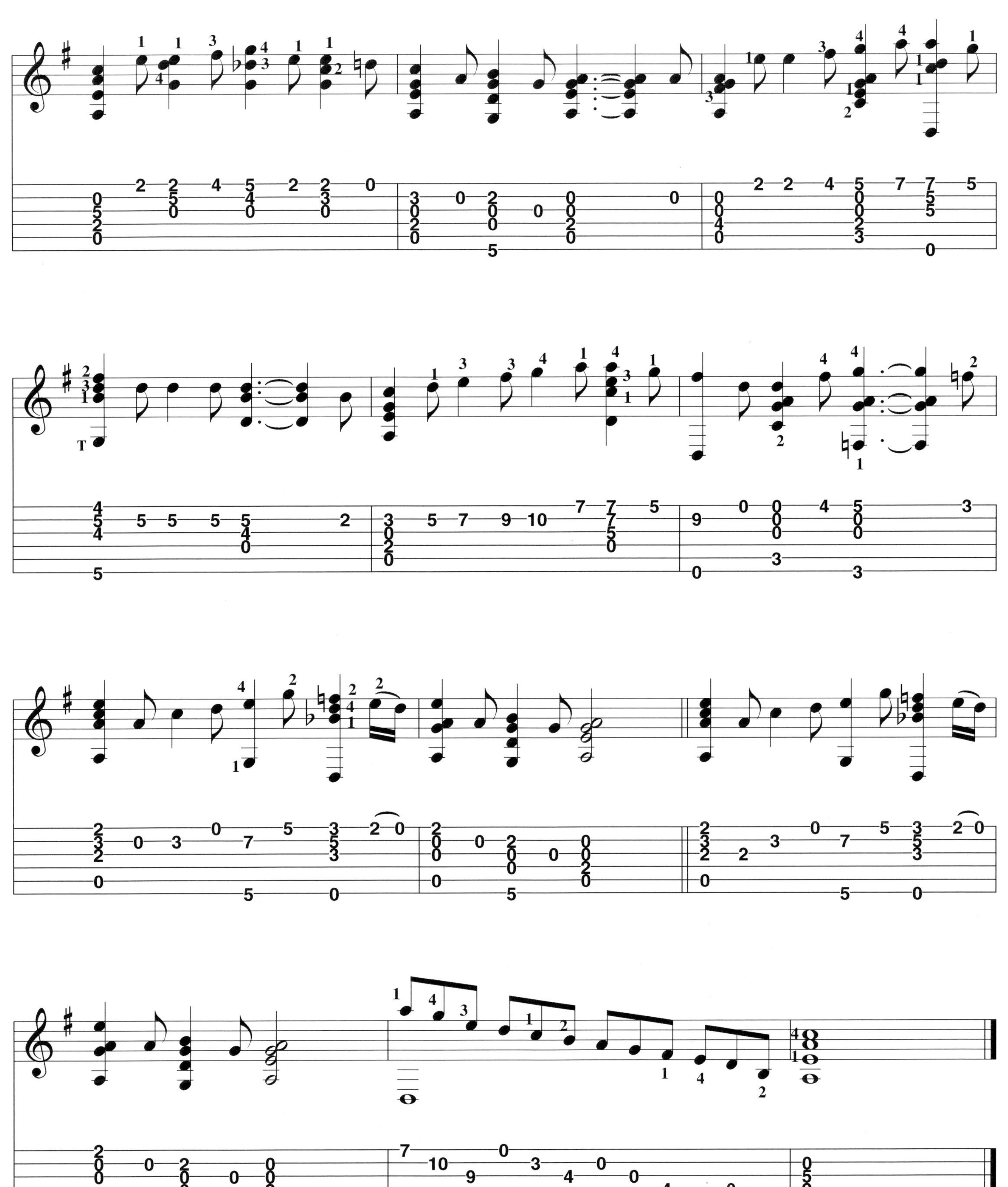

# Salmon Tails Up the Water

This is a great polka and a favourite with Northumbrian pipers.

Technical Notes - Tune the guitar DGDGBE low to high.

The arrangement speaks for itself. The melody is set against an alternating bass. Make the strings buzz and have a good time with this one.

# Salmon Tails Up the Water

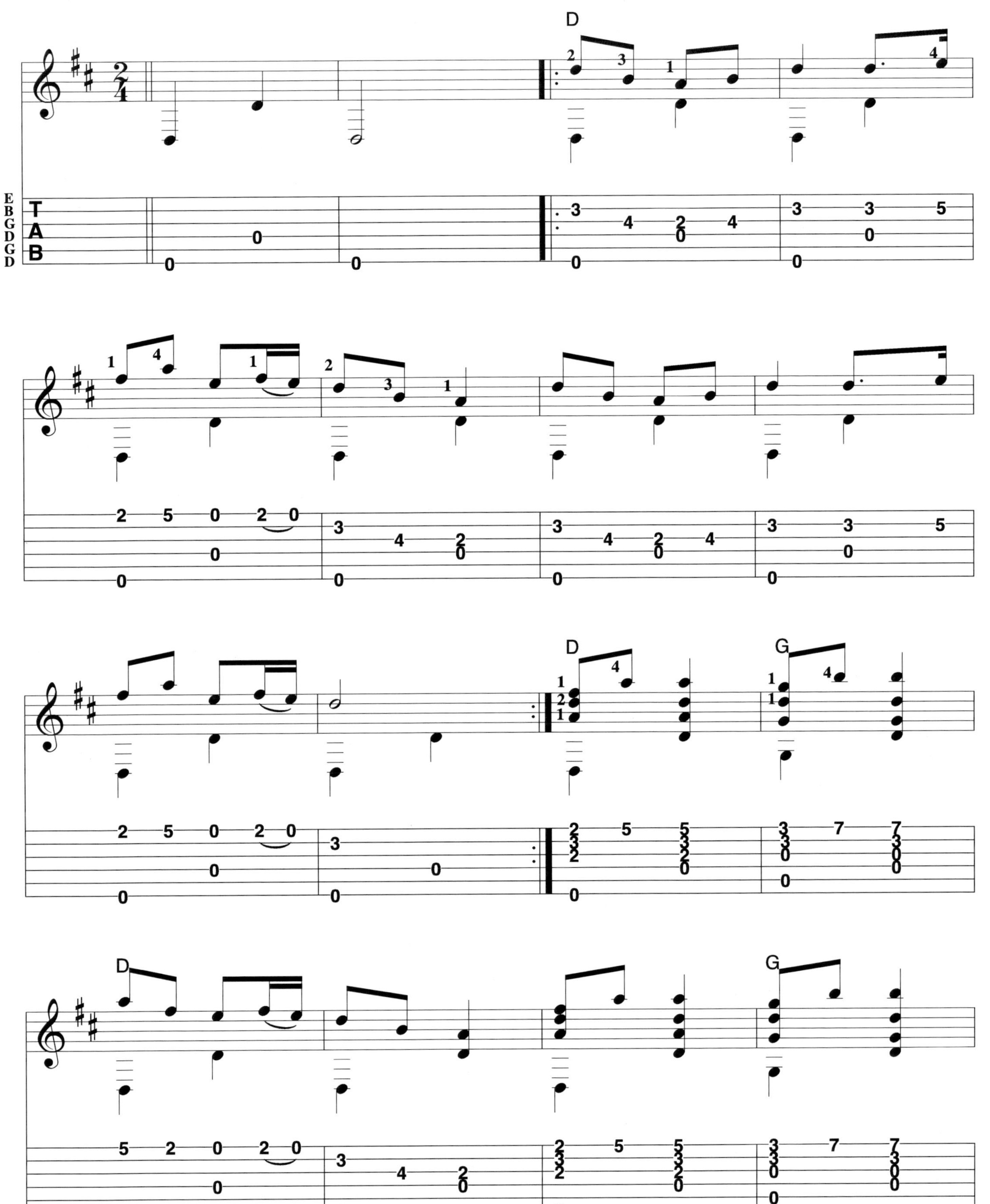

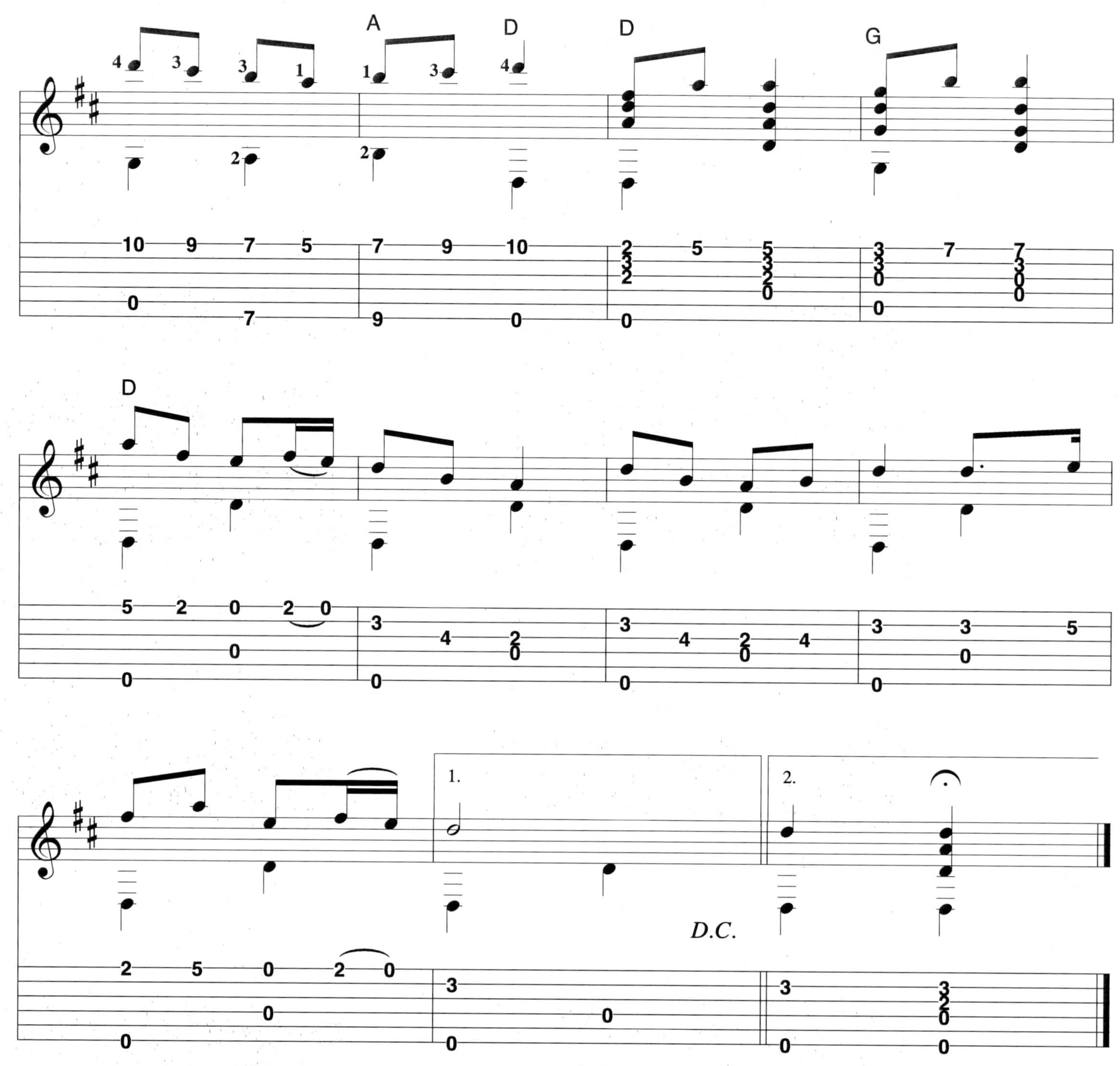
A
D
D
G
D
1.
2.
D.C.

# The Hesleyside Reel

This is a great Northumbrian reel. Hesleyside is an area in Northumberland.

Technical Notes - Tune the guitar DGDGBE low to high.

This tune makes extensive use of finger snaps so take it slowly and build the speed up gradually.

The left hand fingering in bars 3 and 7 could present some difficulty so practice it in small sections.

# The Hesleyside Reel

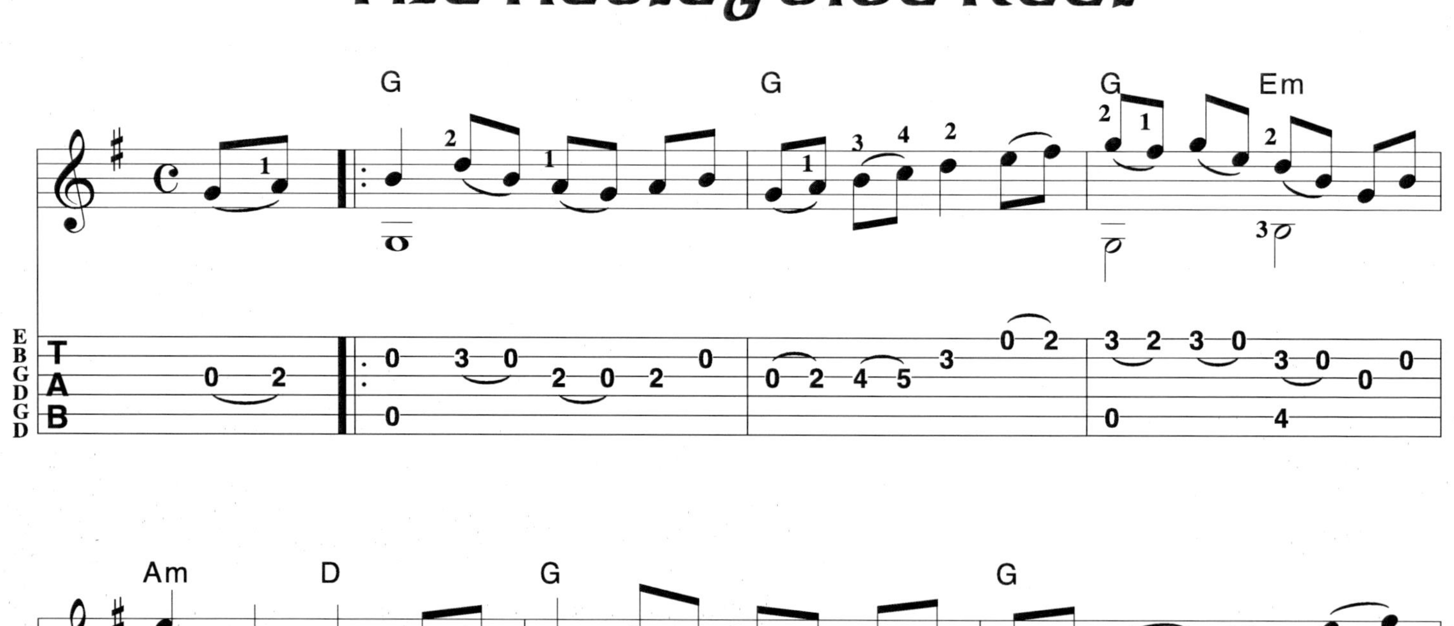


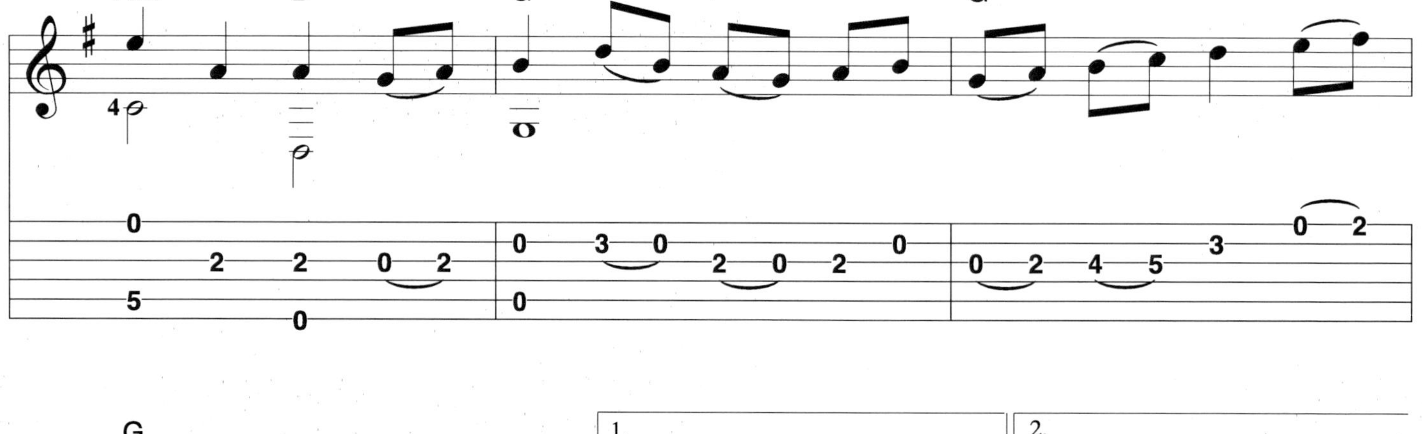


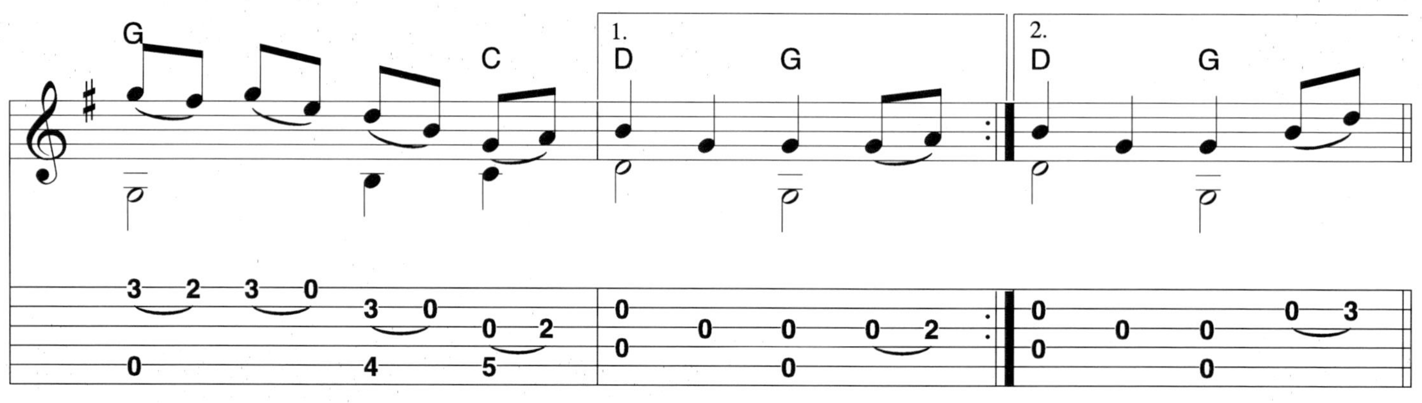


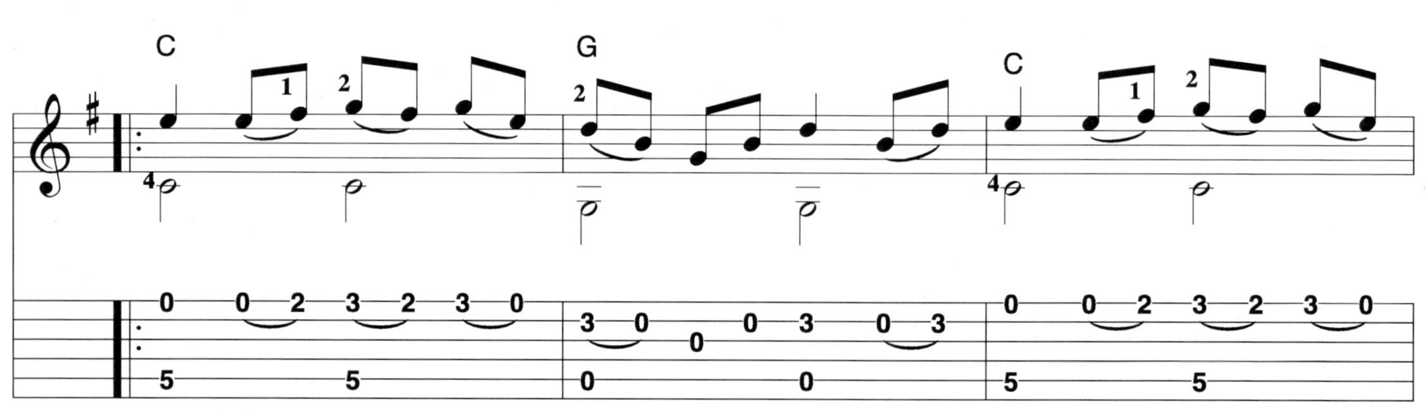

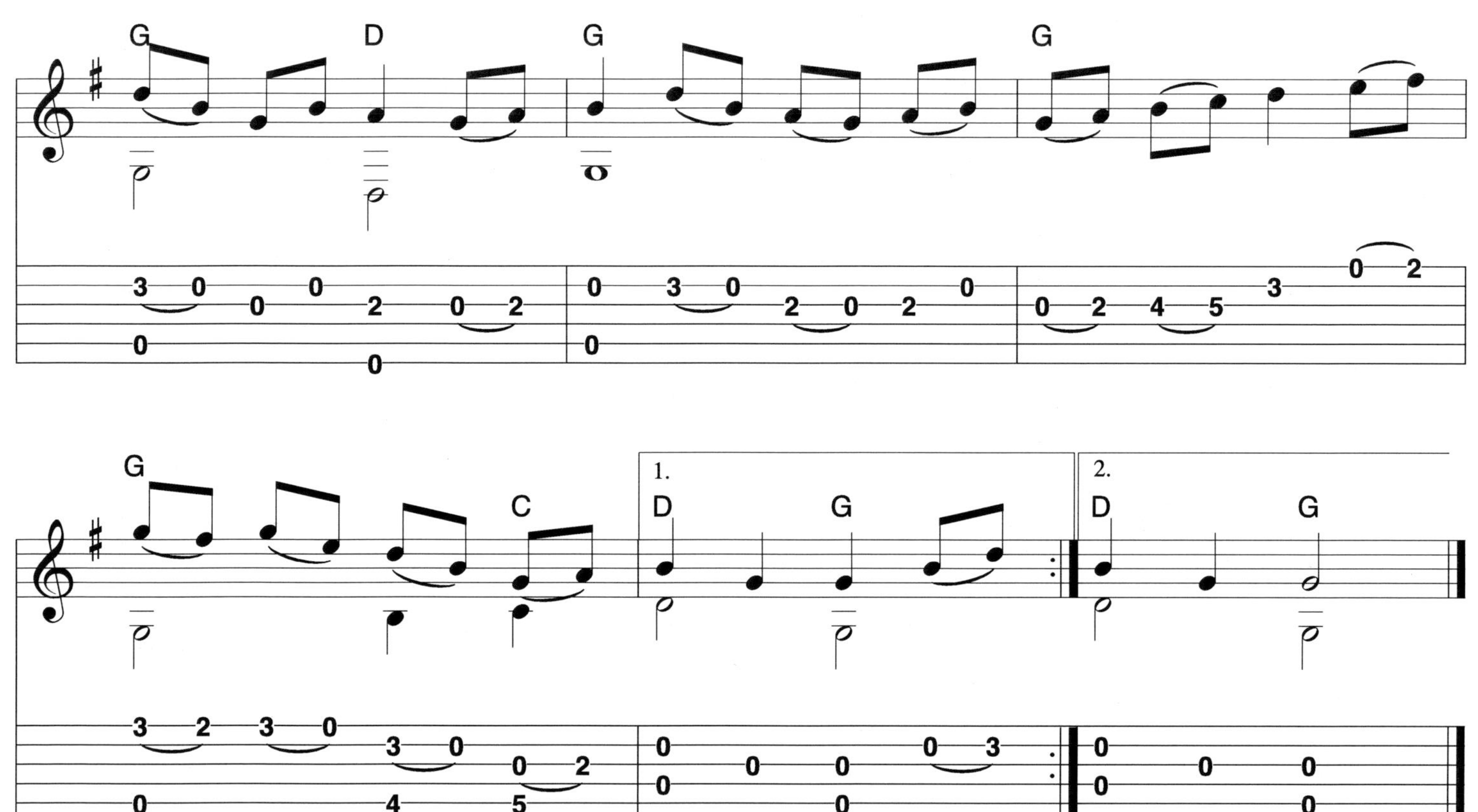
G
D
G
G
G
C
1.
D
G
2.
D
G

# Johnny Armstrong

This is a very old tune written in honour of a famous robber and cut-throat. Johnny Armstrong was hung at Carlenrigg Chapel in the Scottish Borders in 1529 along with 48 of his followers.

Technical Notes - Tune the guitar DADGAD low to high.

Play this tune in a very free manner. Think unaccompanied singer when you play this tune.

# Johnny Armstrong

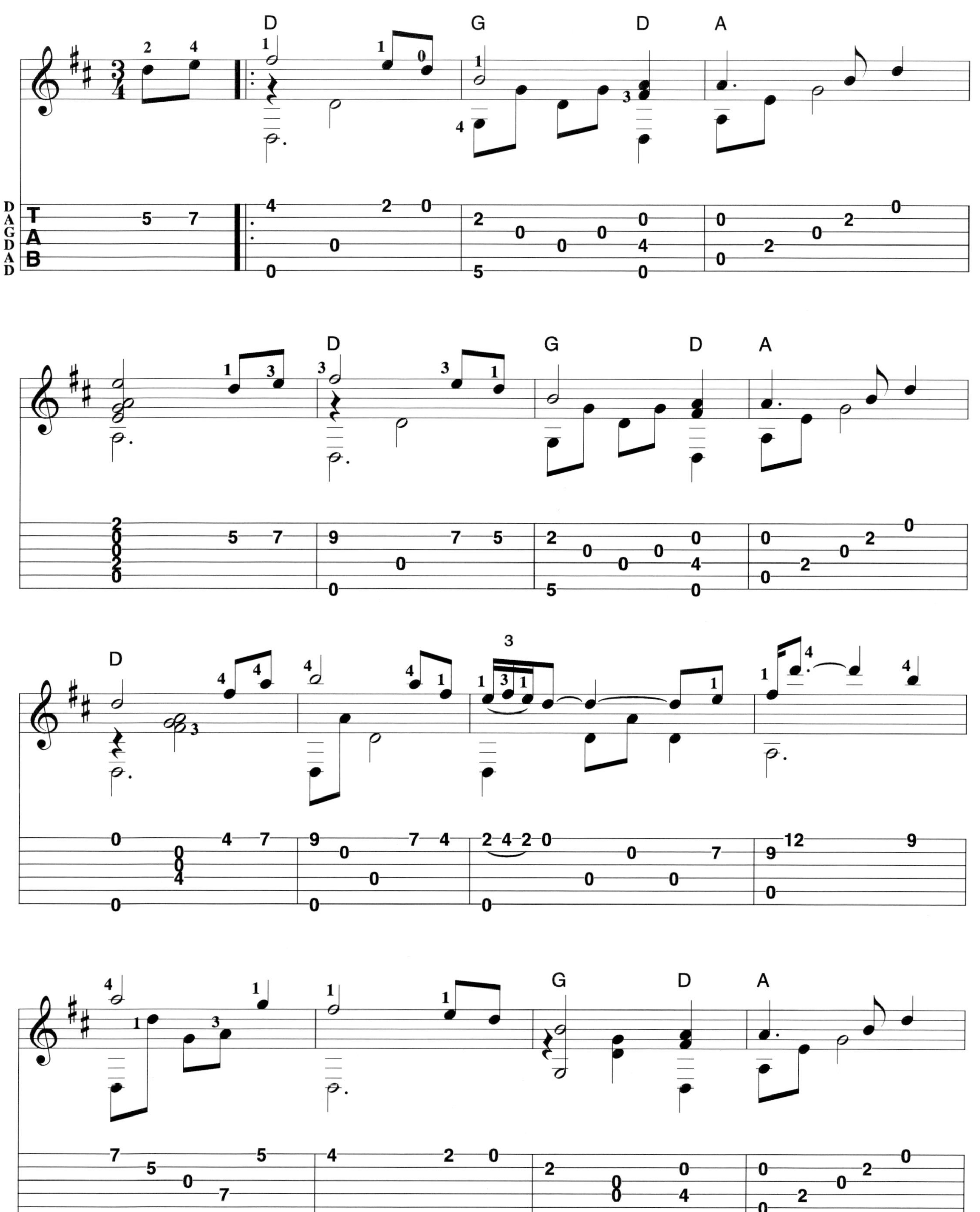

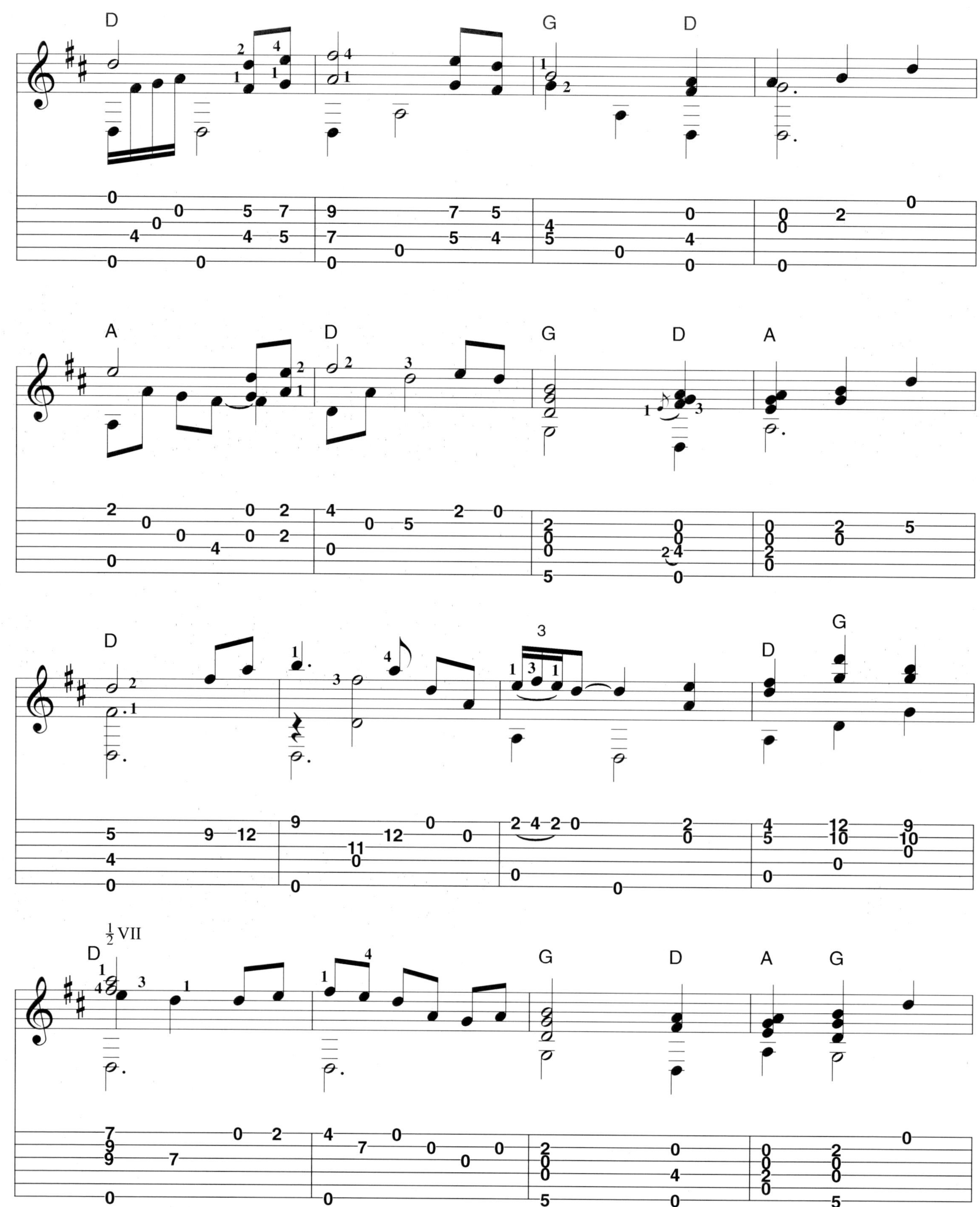
D G D
A D G D A
D D G
½ VII
D G D A G

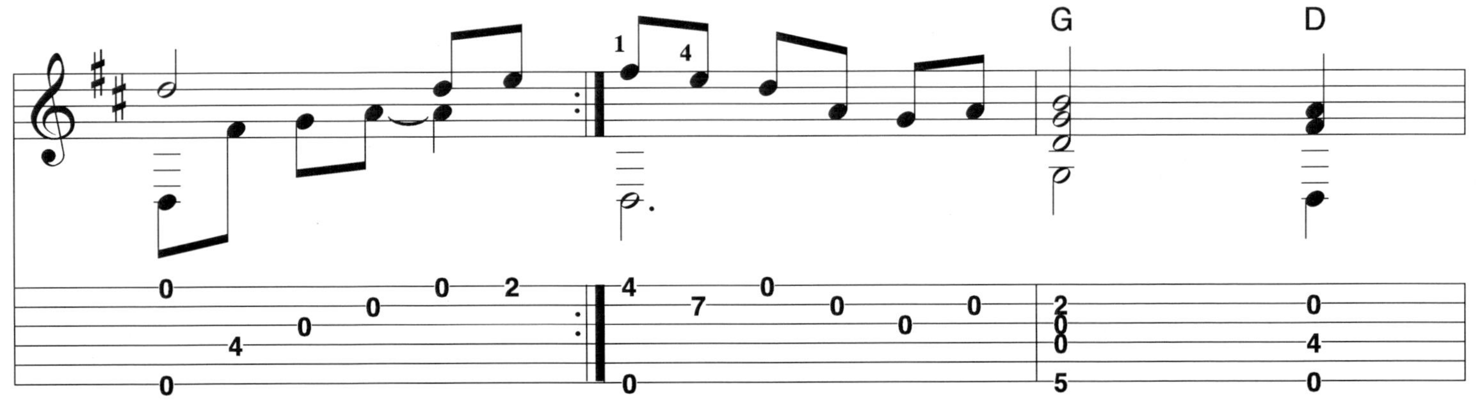
G
D

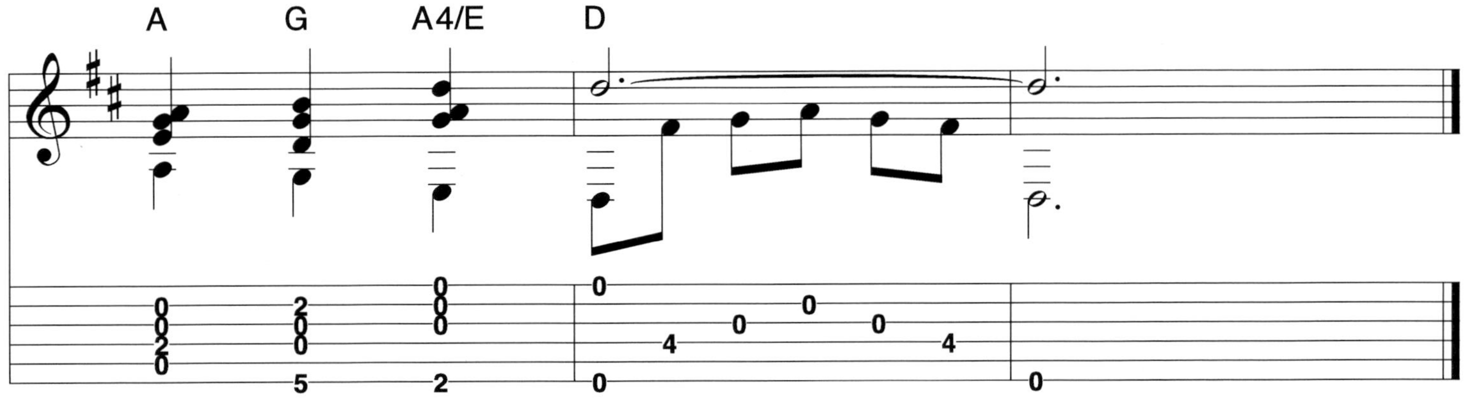
A
G
A4/E
D

# Jimmy Allen

This is another polka tune.

Jimmy Allen (1734-1810), was a virtuoso Northumbrian piper who deserted from the army 9 times, was arrested 13 times and was a bigamist 3 times.

Technical Notes - Tune the guitar DGDGBE low to high.

The first section of this tune is fairly straightforward with the melody set against the alternating bass.

The section can be a bit tricky. Follow the left hand fingering carefully in the first three bars and be careful of the stretch in the 3rd bar.

If stretches like this are a problem, try fingering them in the higher positions and moving down the fingerboard fret by fret.

Be prepared to be rough and ready with this tune.

# Jimmy Allen

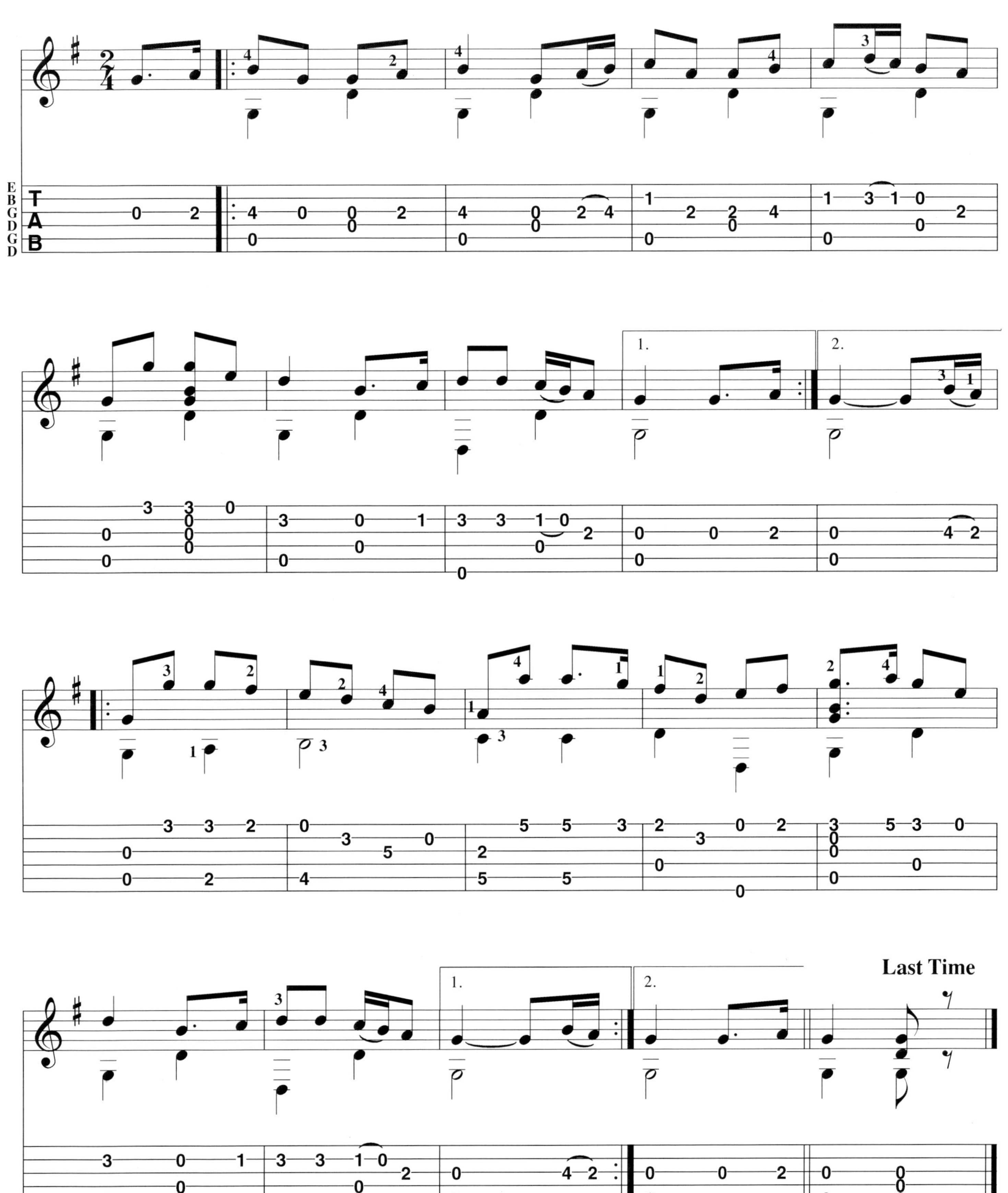

# Felton Lonnen

Felton is a village in Northumberland. Lonnen is the Northumbrian name for a lane.

Technical Notes - Tune the guitar DGDGAD low to high.

When playing passages with right hand harmonics, use the index finger and thumb to play the harmonic and the 3rd or 4th fingers to play the melody.

# Felton Lonnen

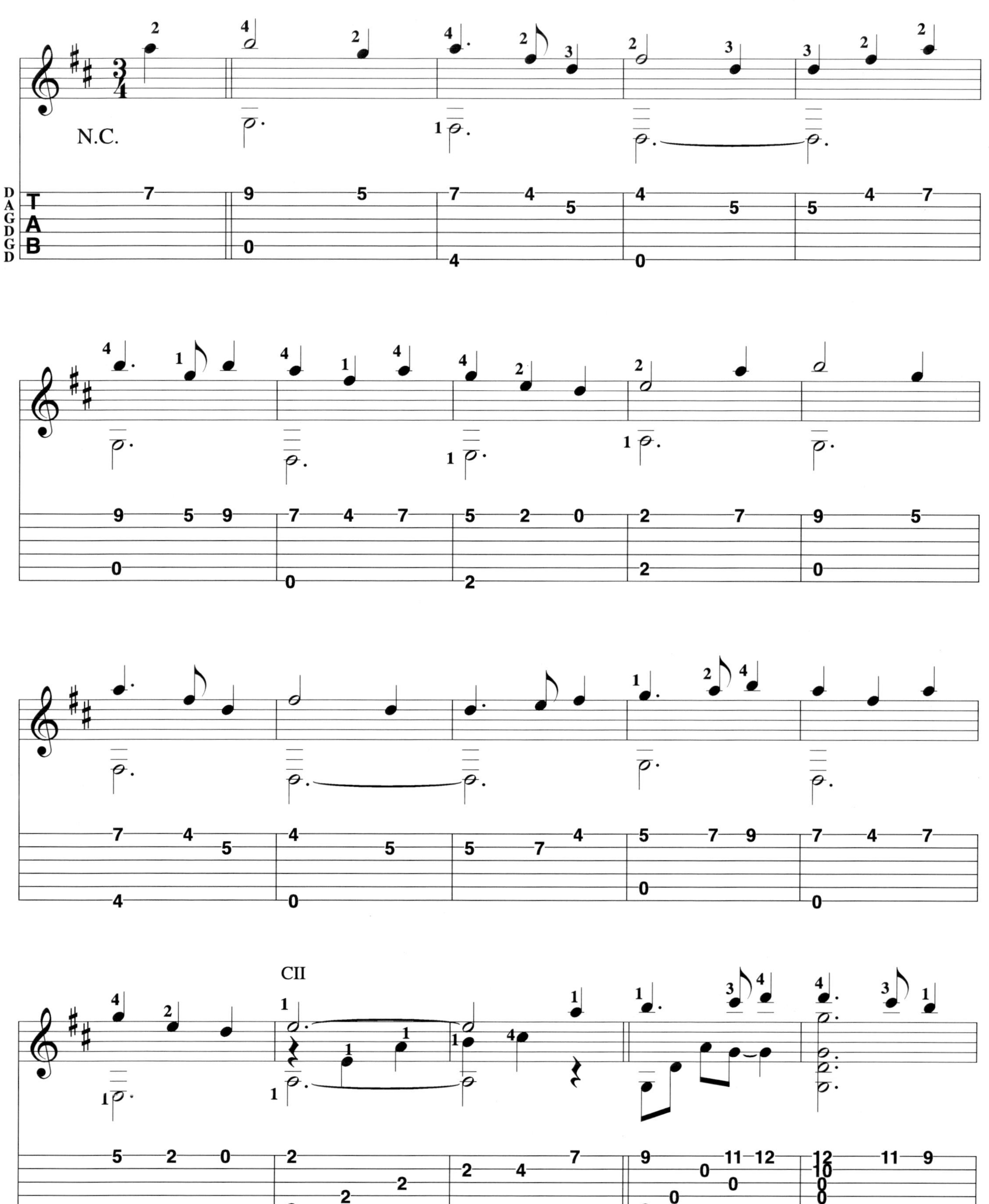

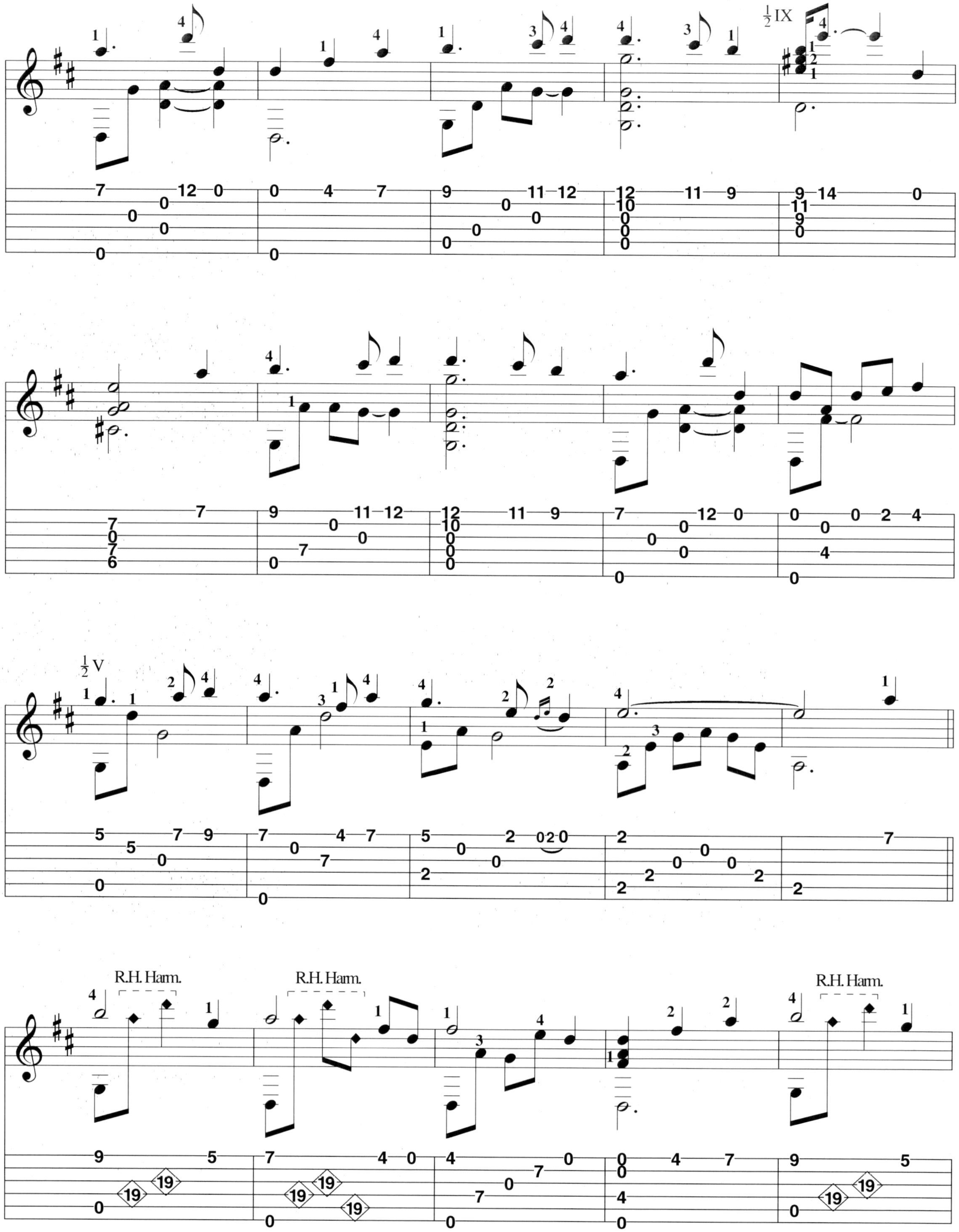

$\frac{1}{2}$ IX

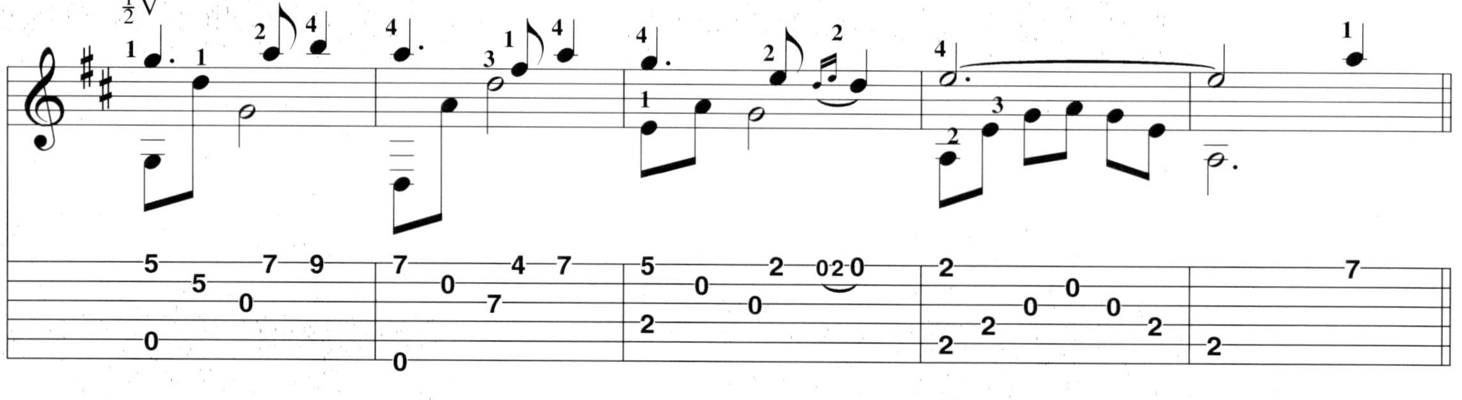


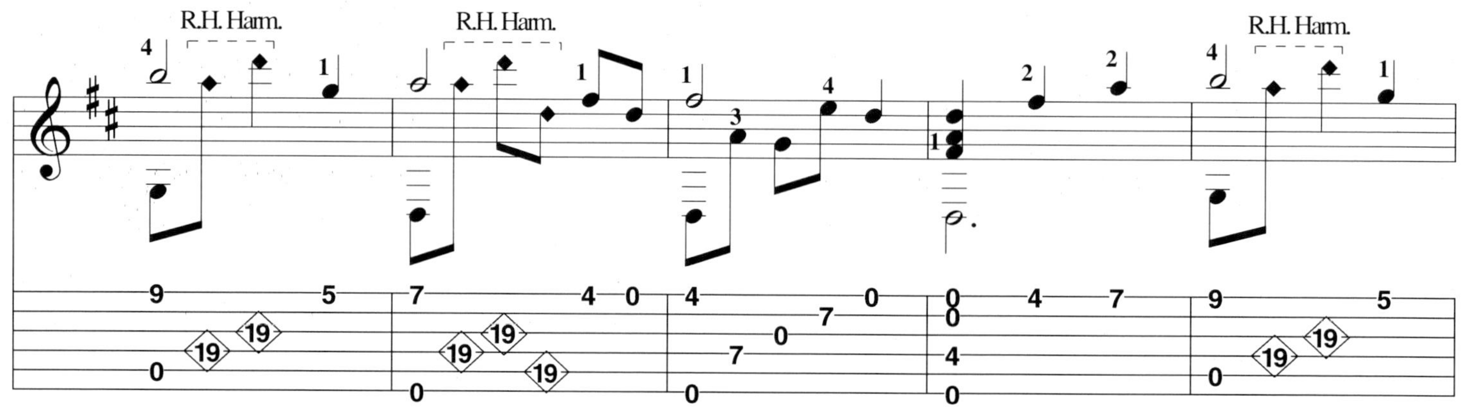

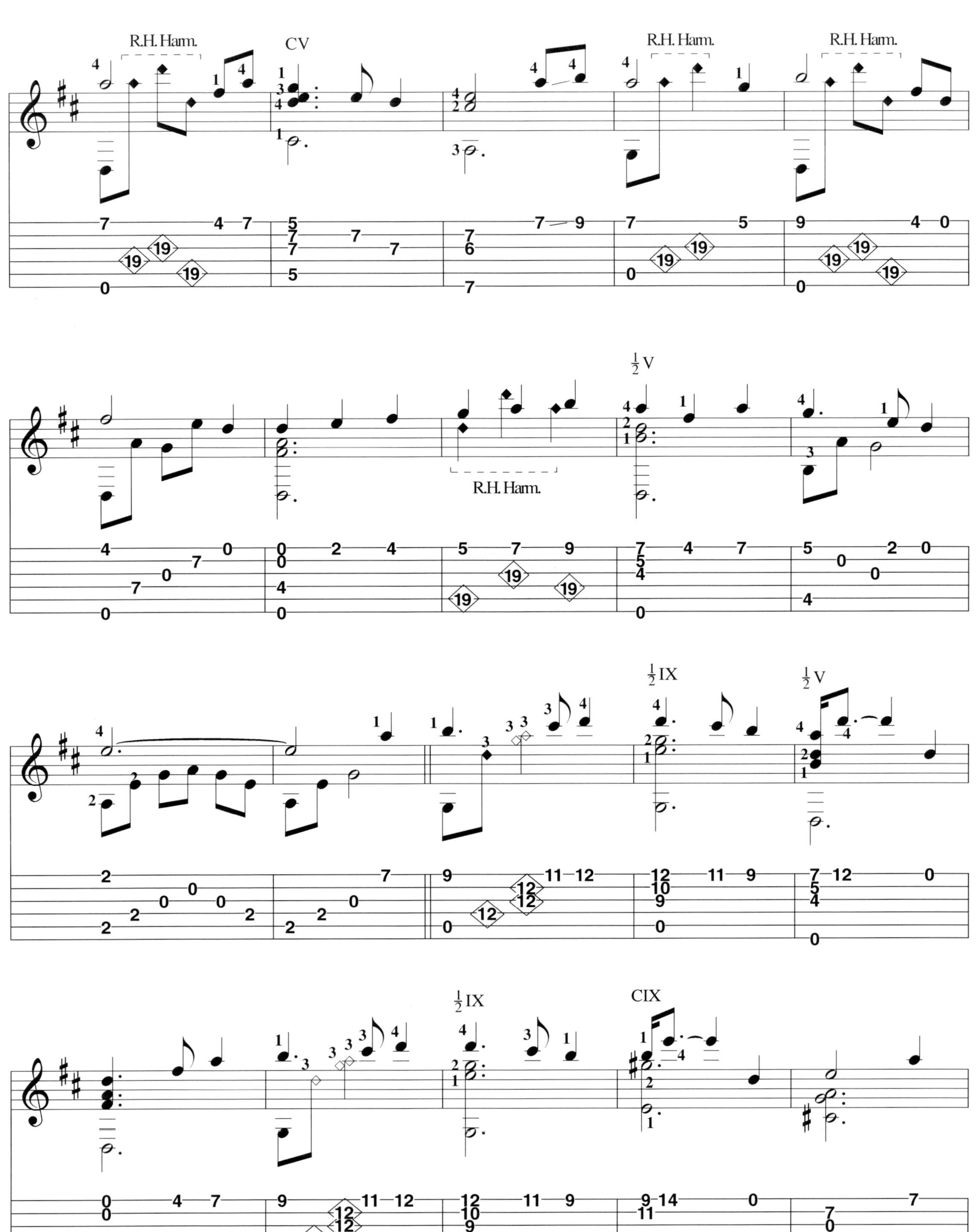

R.H. Harm.
CV
R.H. Harm.
R.H. Harm.
½ V
R.H. Harm.
½ IX
½ V
½ IX
CIX

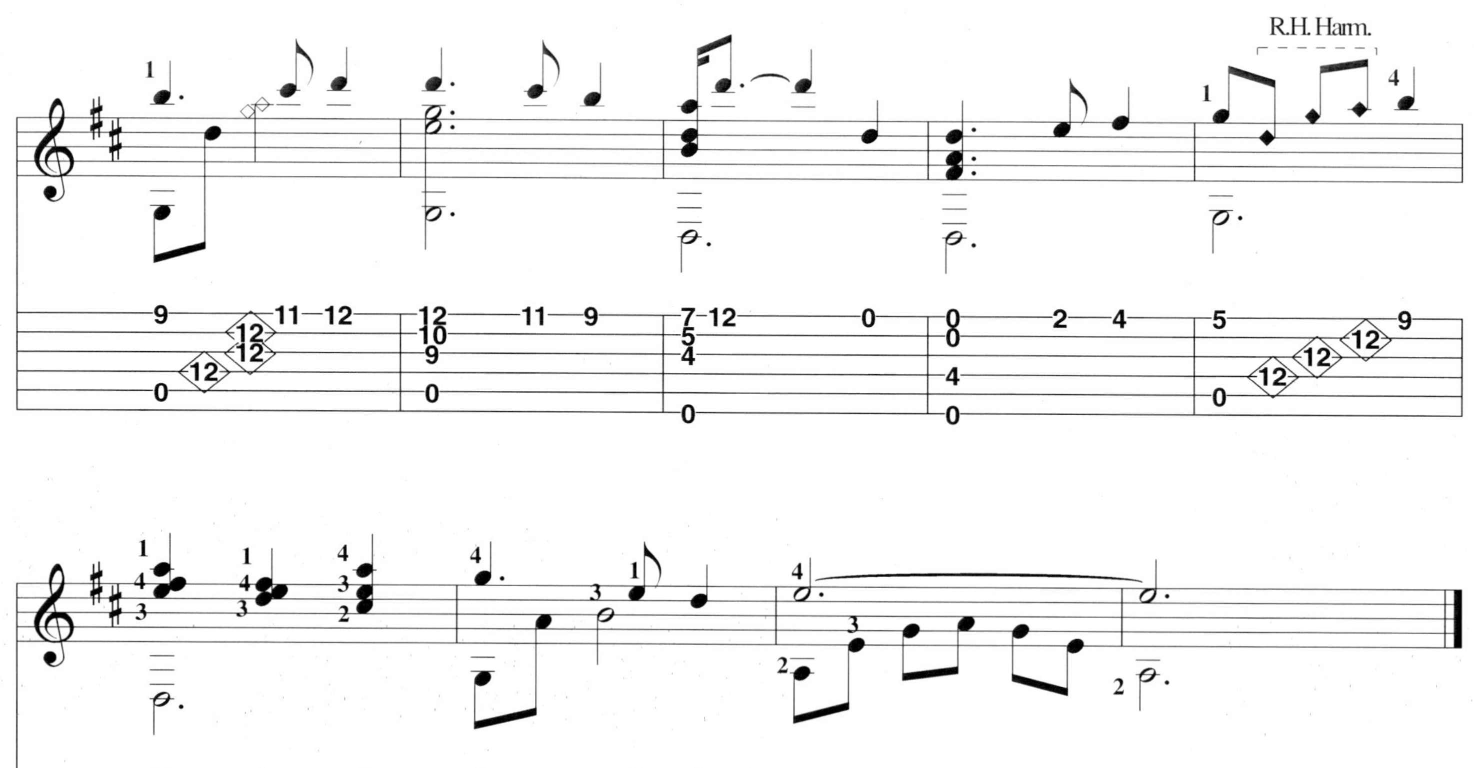
R.H. Harm.

# Sir John Fenwick

This tune dates from the Jacobite period. Sir John Fenwick was a noted Northumbrian Jacobite who was dispossessed of his lands.

Technical Notes - Tune the guitar DGDGAD low to high.

For the cross-string melody notes, try to keep the left hand fingers on for as long as possible to give it a harp-like sound.

# Sir John Fenwick

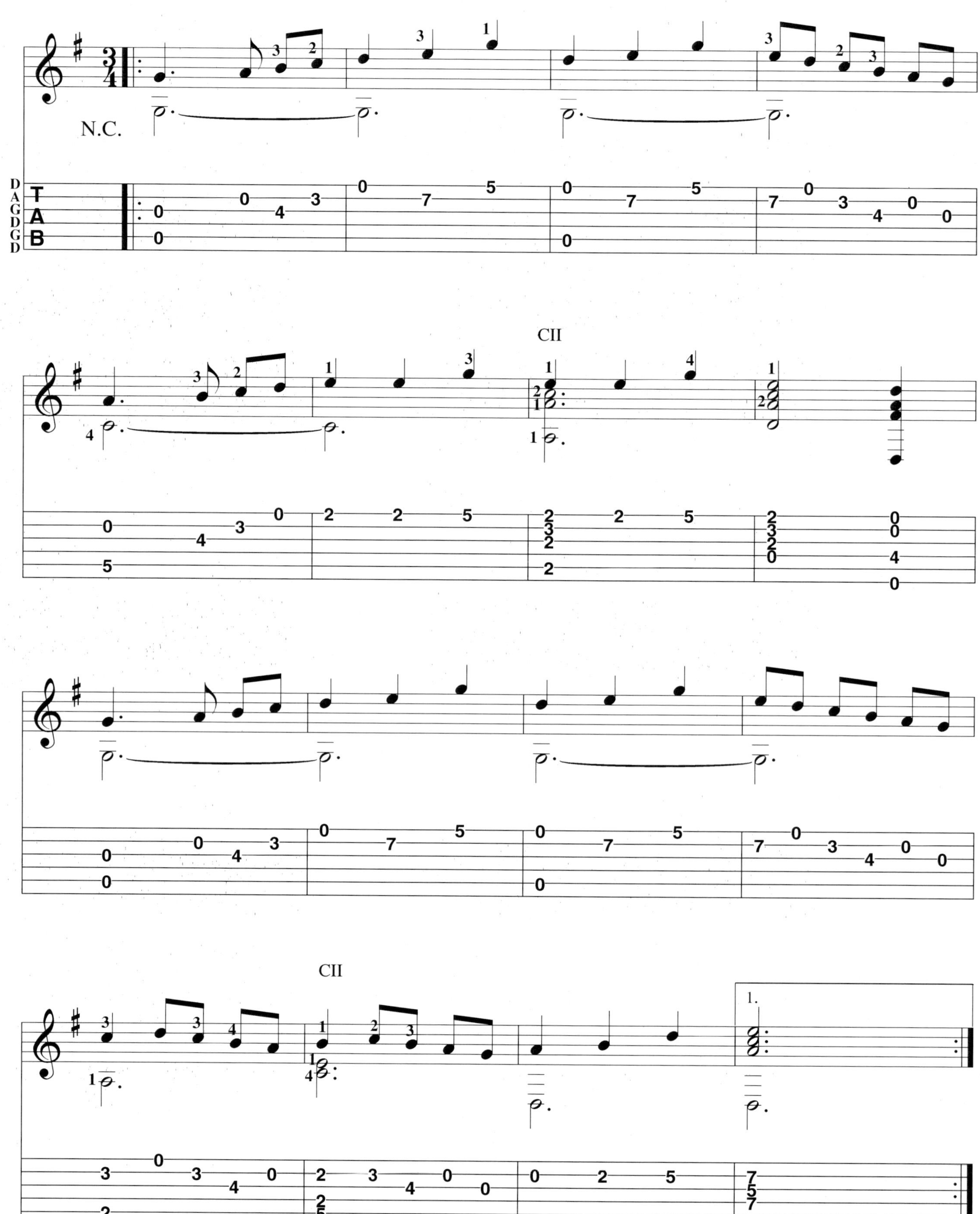

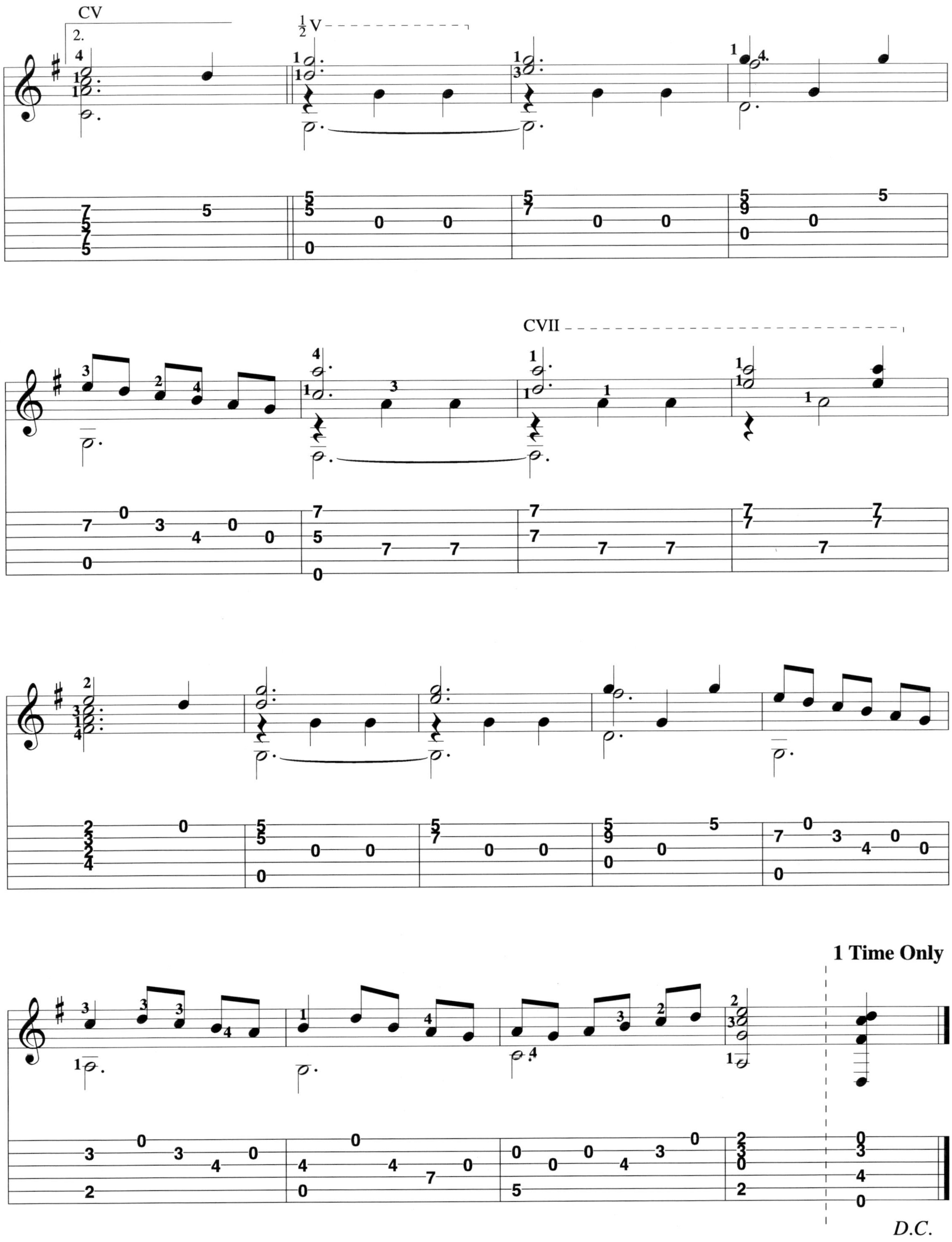

CV

2.

½ V

CVII

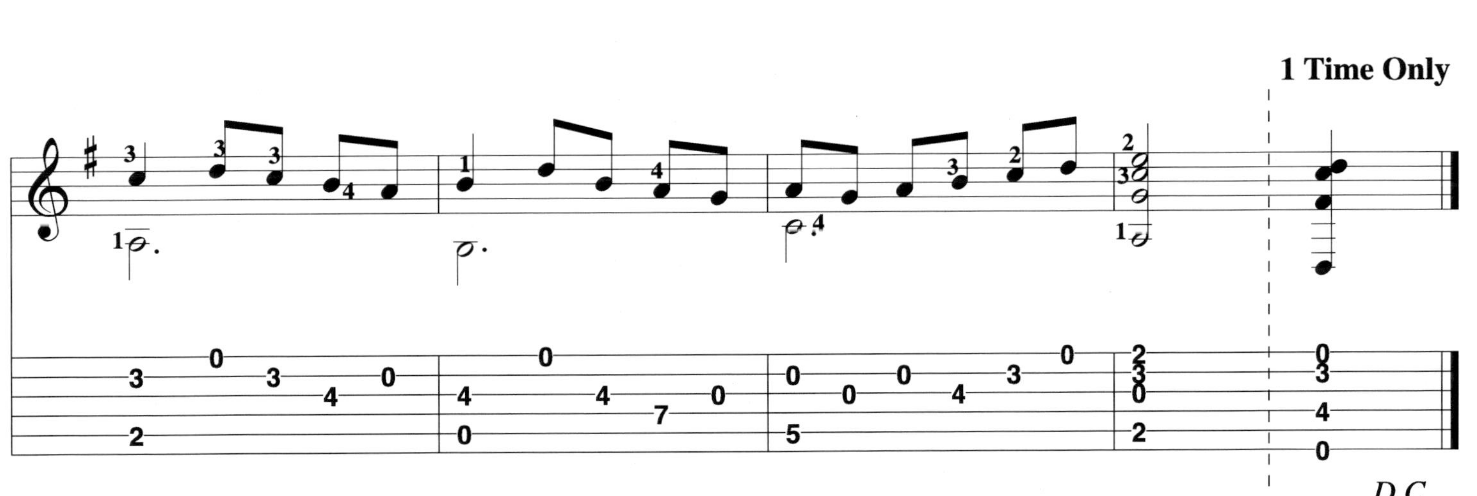

# Bonny Gallowgate Lad

This is a Newcastle street song. Gallowgate is an area within the city of Newcastle.

Technical Notes - Tune the guitar in standard tuning.

There's quite a bit of movement in this one so take it slow and practice it in small sections.

Play it freely.

# Bonny Gallowgate Lad

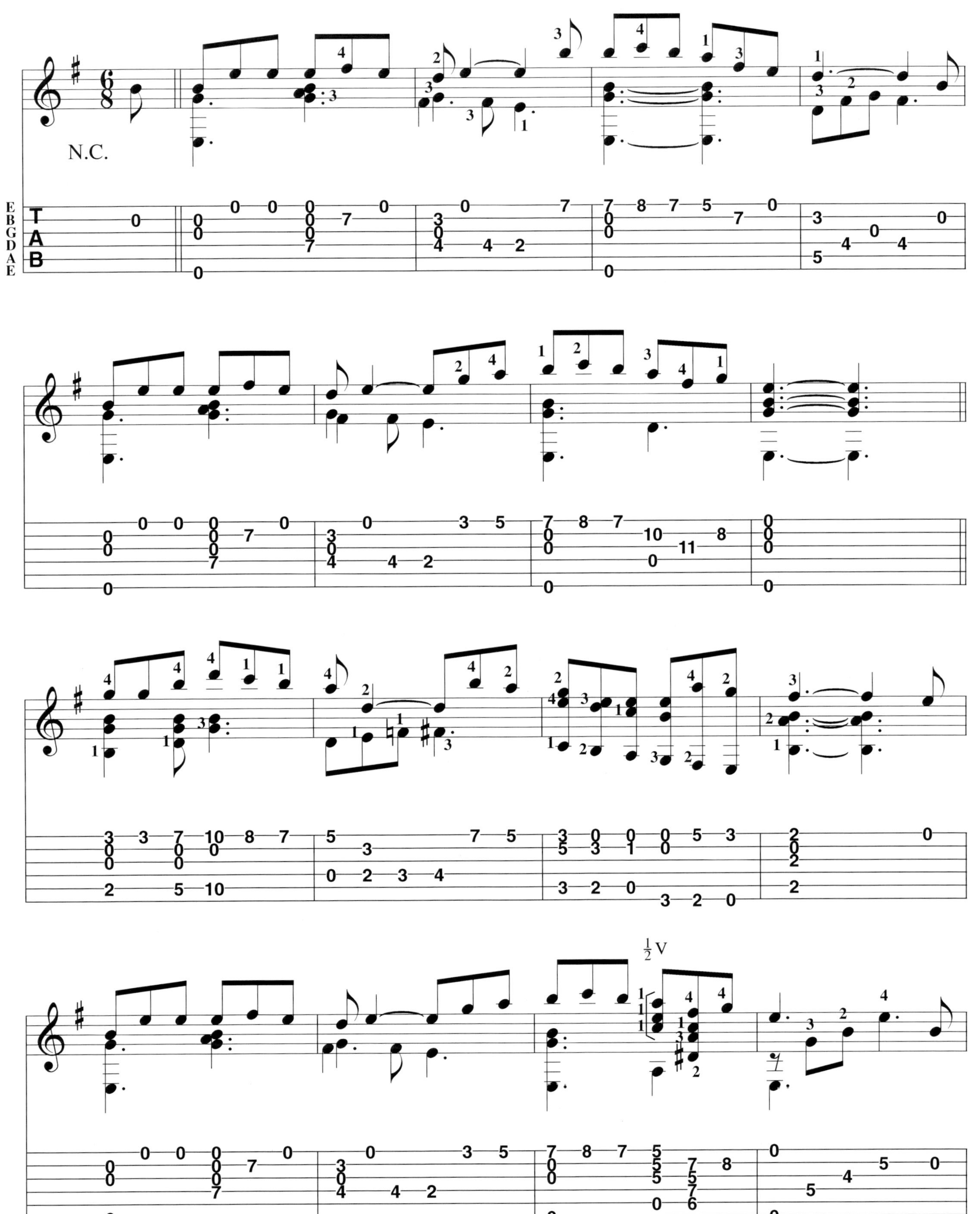

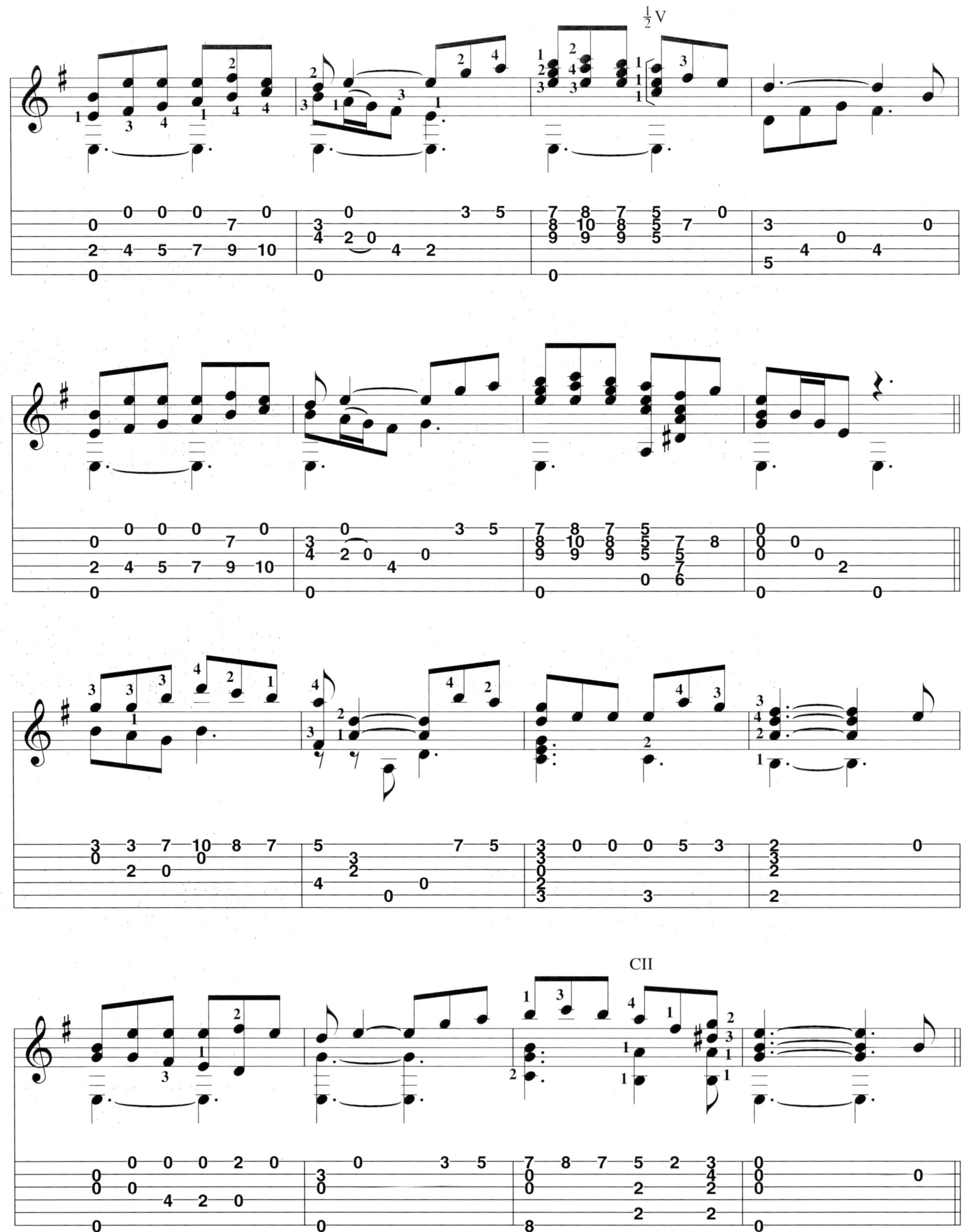
½ V
CII

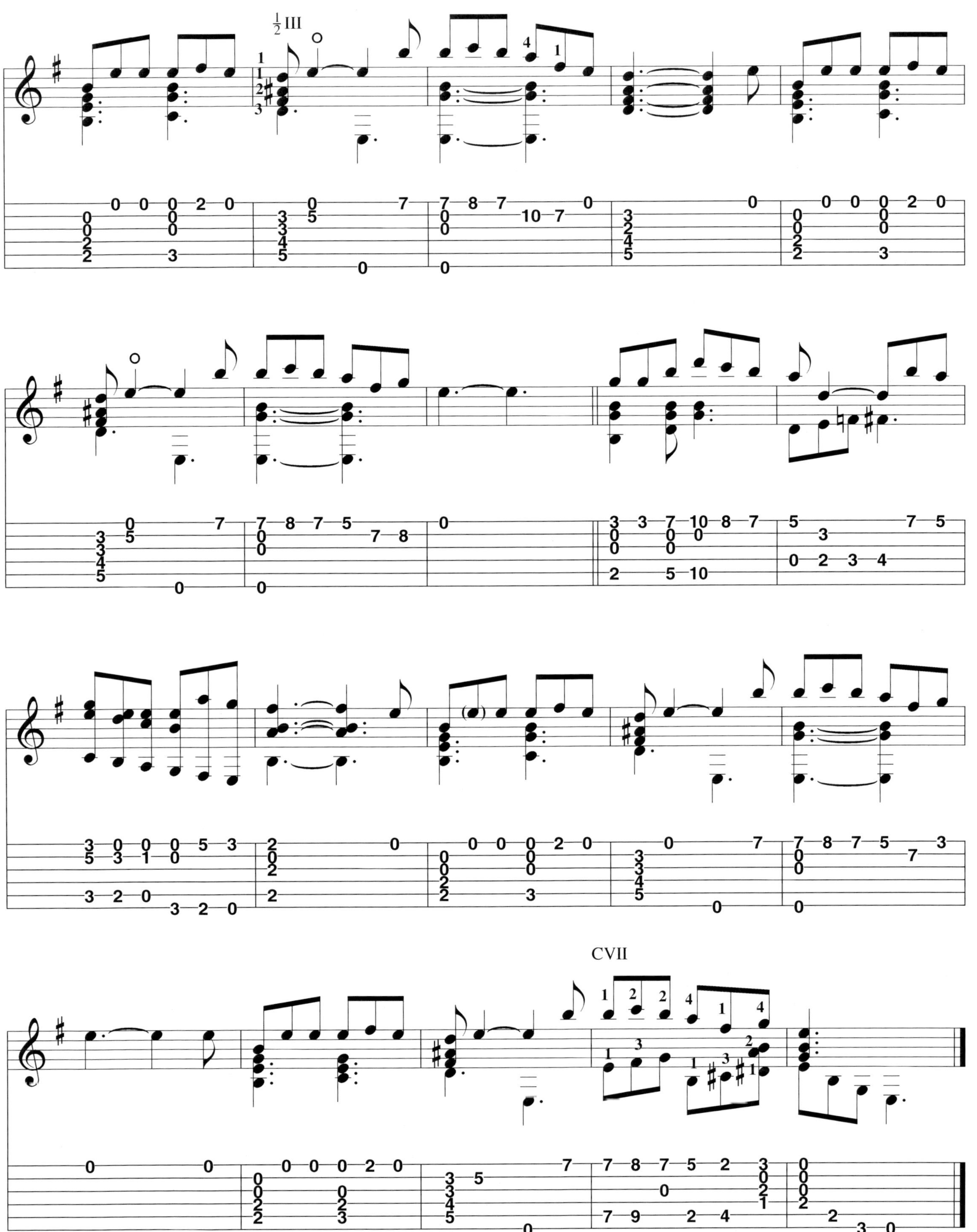
½ III
CVII

# Buy Broom Besoms

This song was written by the Newcastle fiddler "Blind Willie" Purvis (1752 - 1832).

Technical Notes - Tune the guitar in standard tuning.

For the contrary motion passages (bars 9 - 12) use the fingering that's provided. Take it slowly one bit at a time. If you find it difficult you're probably trying to do too much at once.

# Buy Broom Besoms

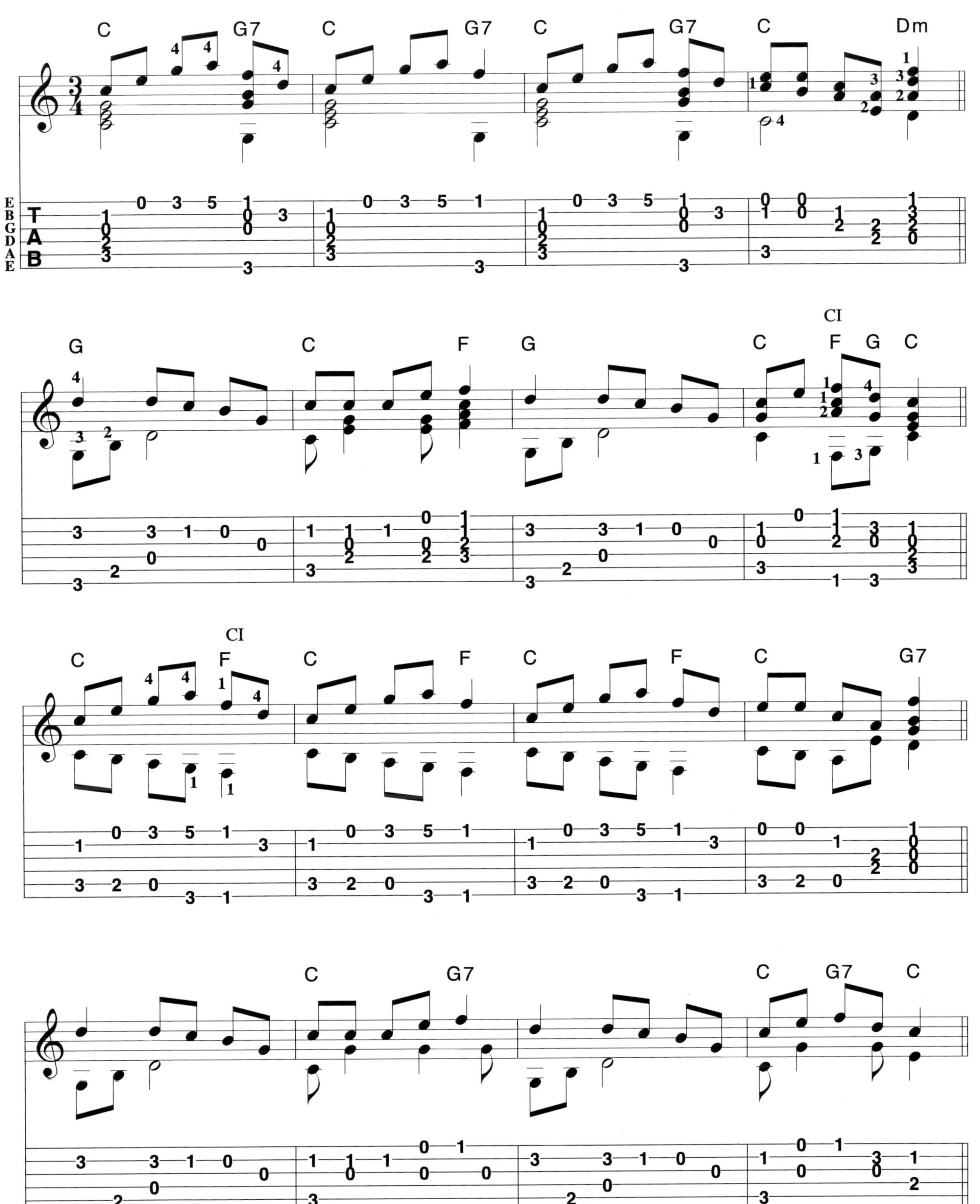

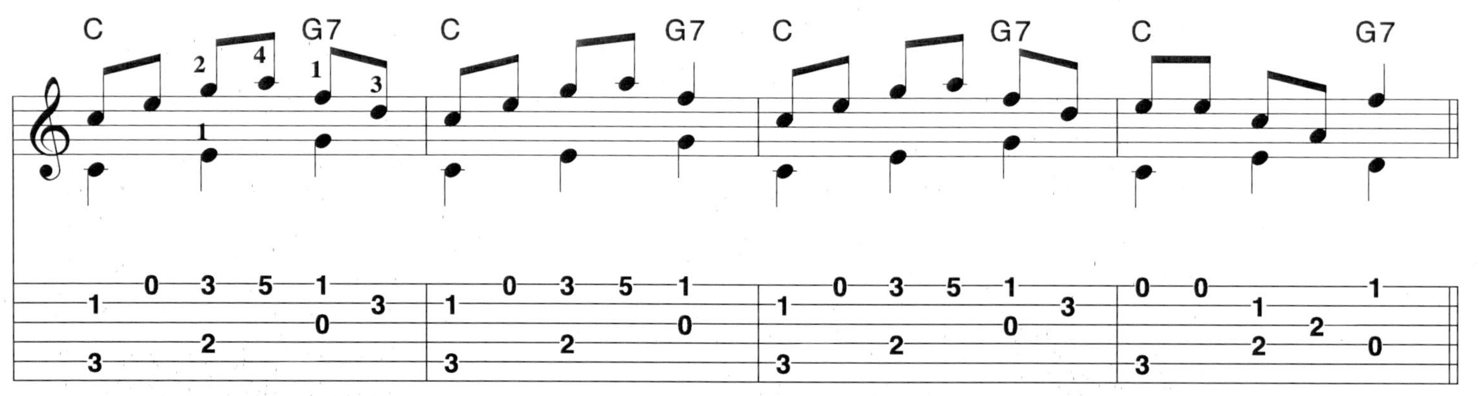
C G7 C G7 C G7 C G7

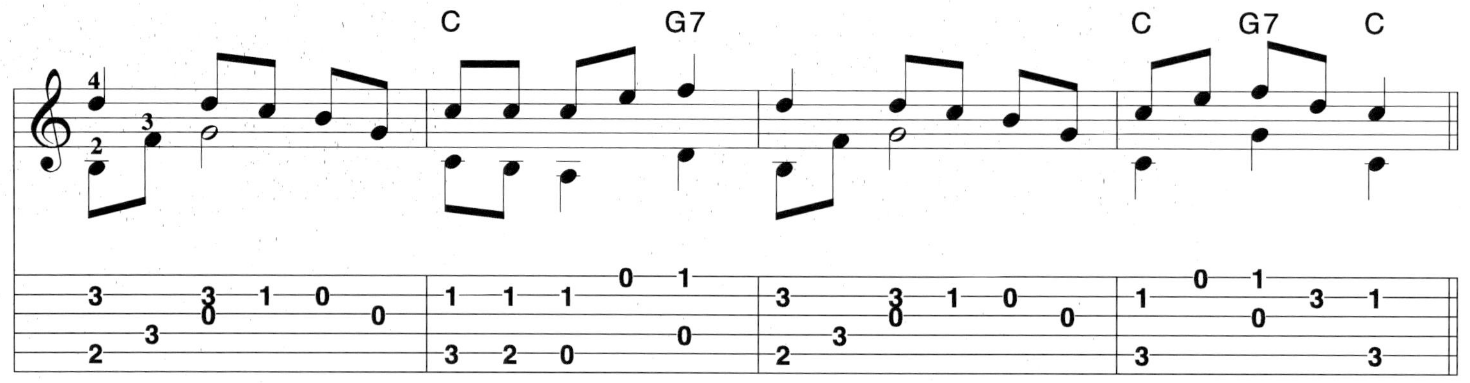
C G7 C G7 C

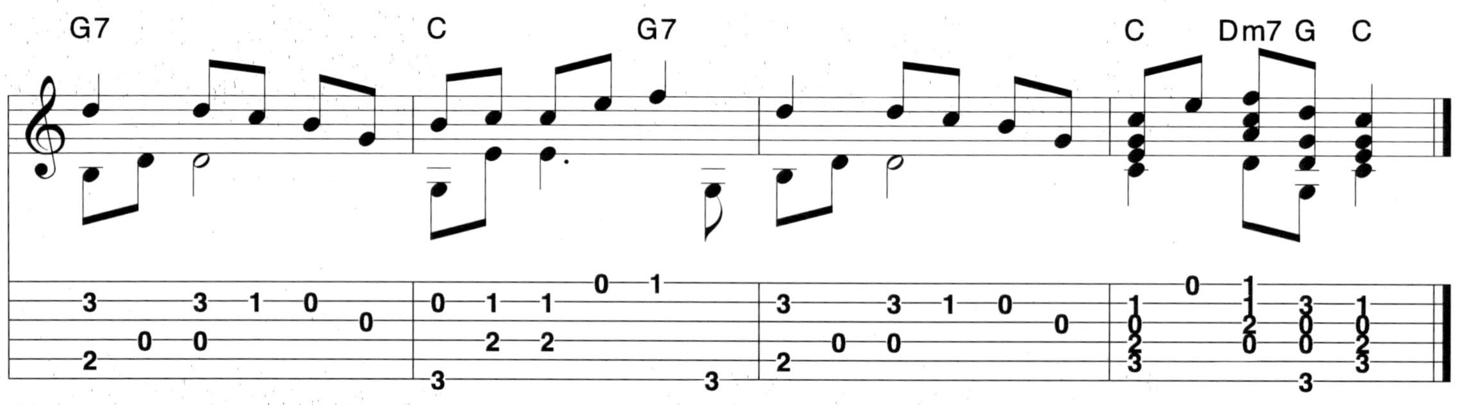
G7 C G7 C Dm7 G C

# Elsie Marley

This tune is a great favourite of mine and very popular throughout North East England.

Technical Notes - Tune the guitar DGDGBE low to high.

The middle section of the tune can be tricky especially the 1st chord in the second time bar. If you're not used to this kind of stretch and find it impossible, forget about the 1st finger A sand play the open G. This will sound OK.

# Elsie Marley

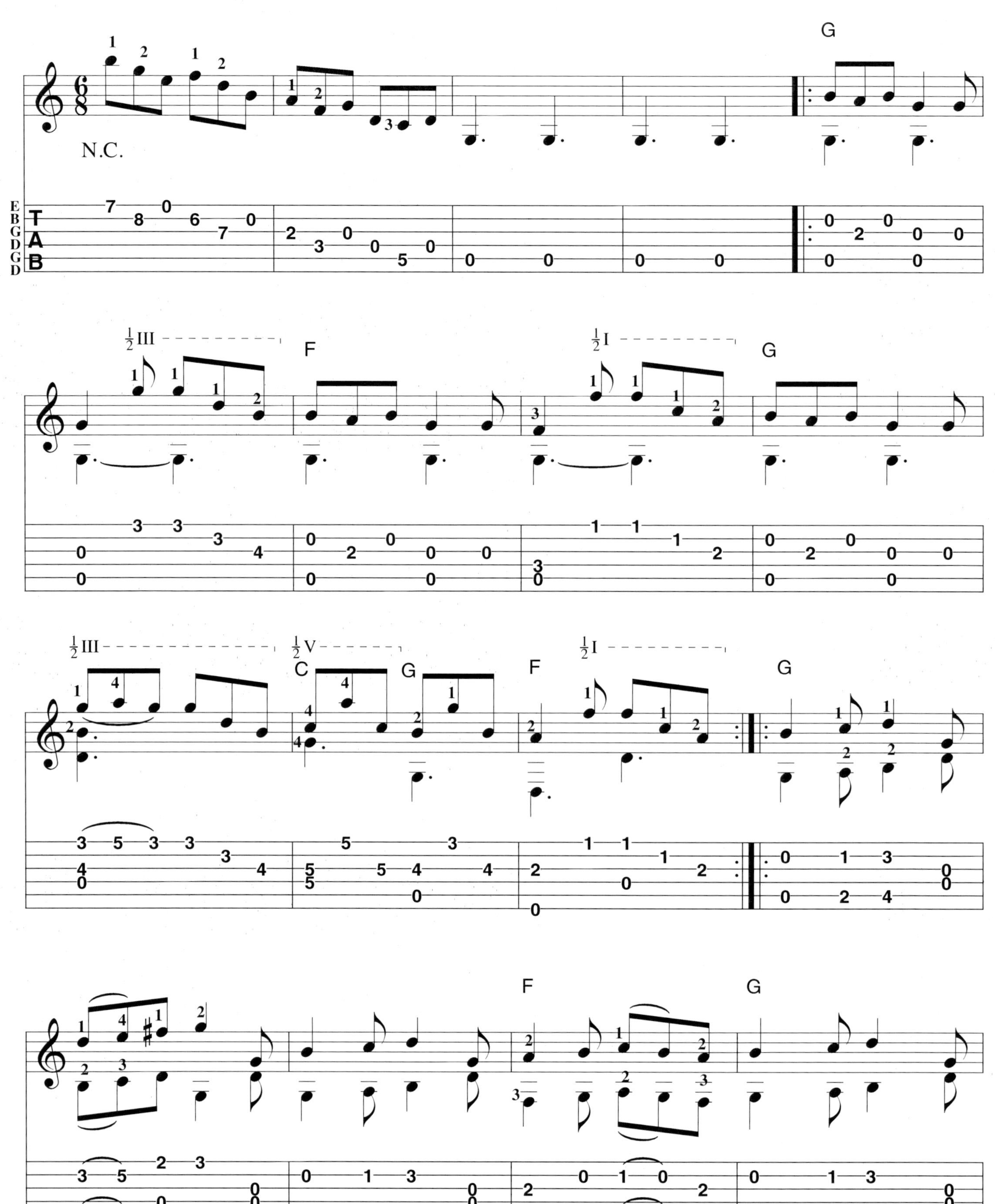

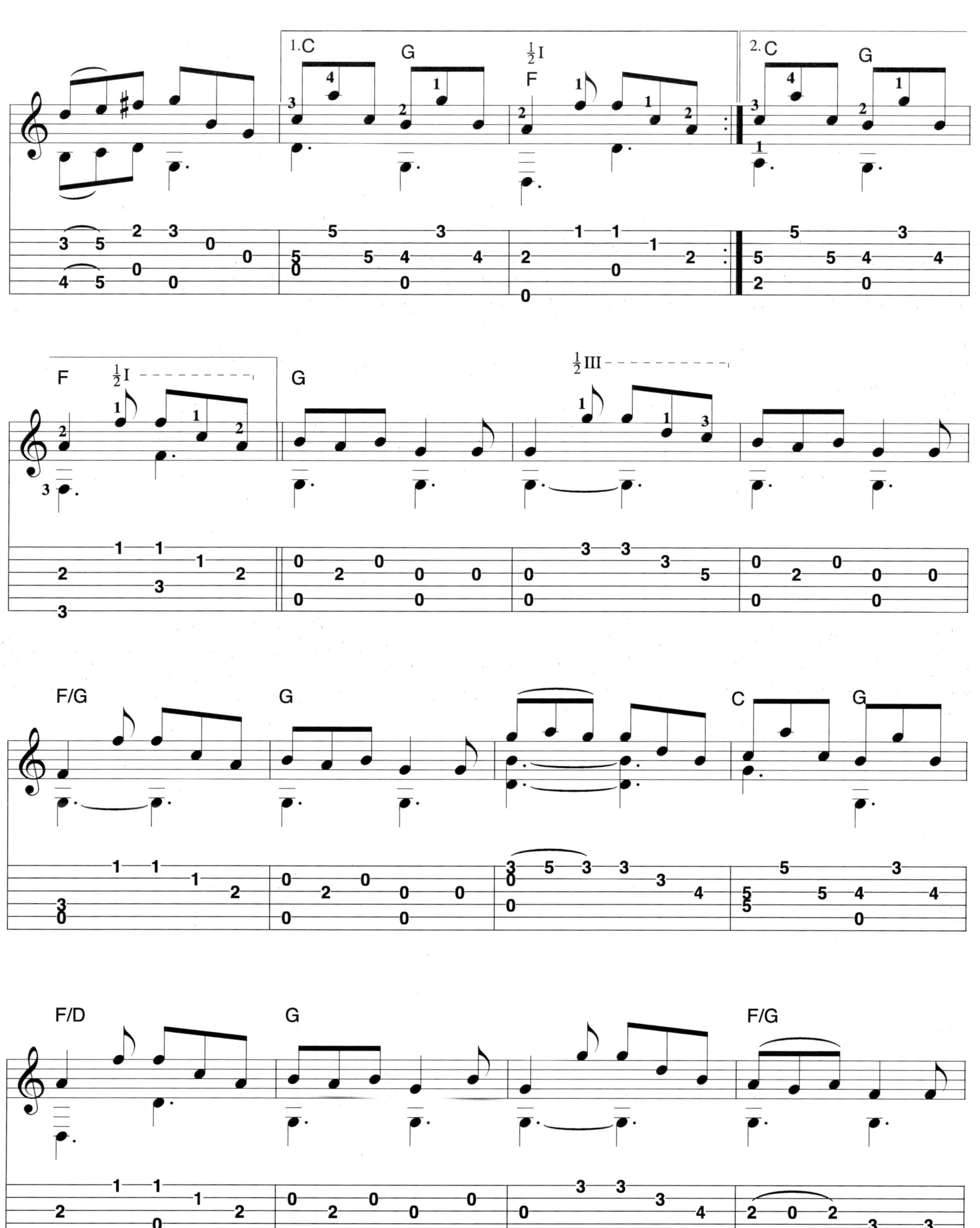
1.C
G
½ I
F
2.C
G
F
½ I
G
½ III
F/G
G
C
G
F/D
G
F/G

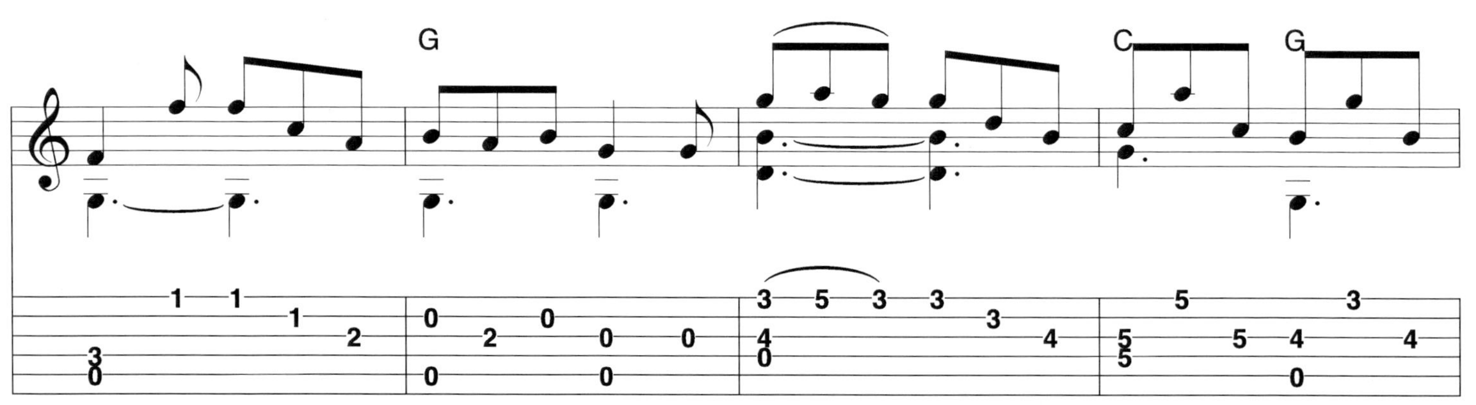
G
C
G

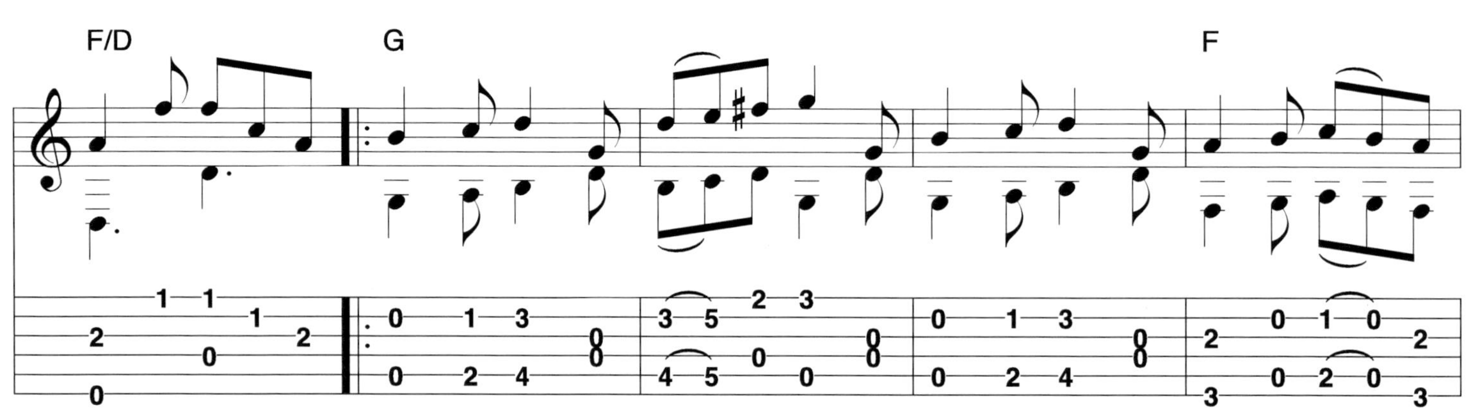
F/D
G
F

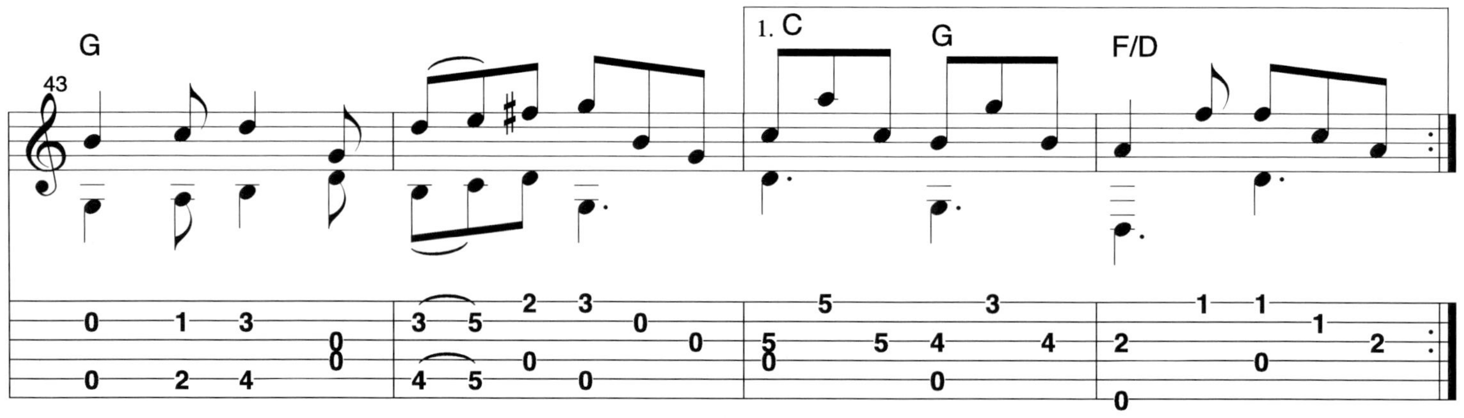
G
43
1. C
G
F/D

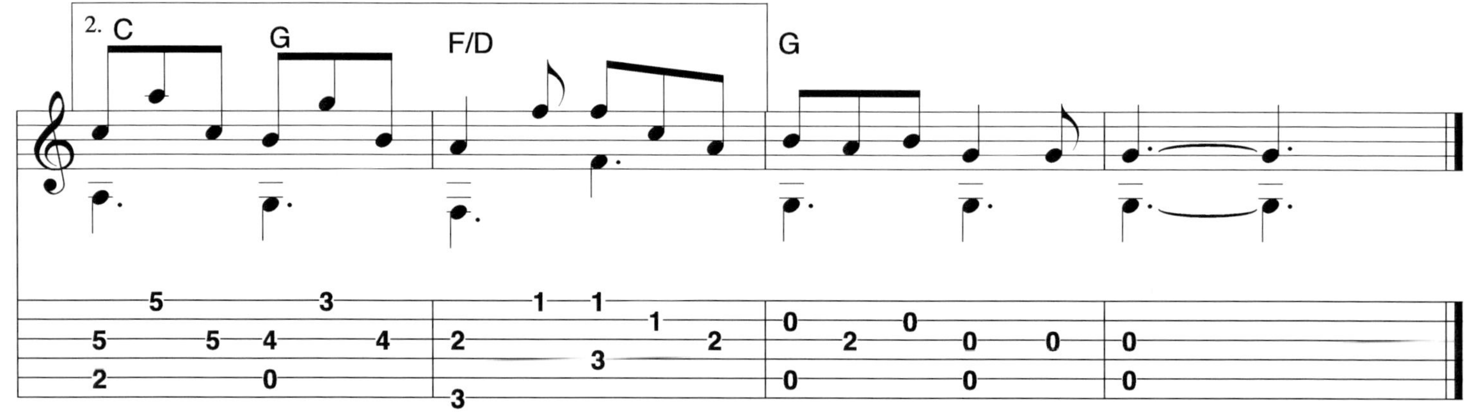
2. C
G
F/D
G

# Sweet Hesleyside

This is a beautiful Northumbrian pipe tune.

Technical Notes - Tune the guitar DGDGBE low to high.

The right hand fingering I use is as follows:

- 3rd finger for melody notes.
- Thumb, index and middle fingers for the accompaniment notes.

# Sweet Hesleyside

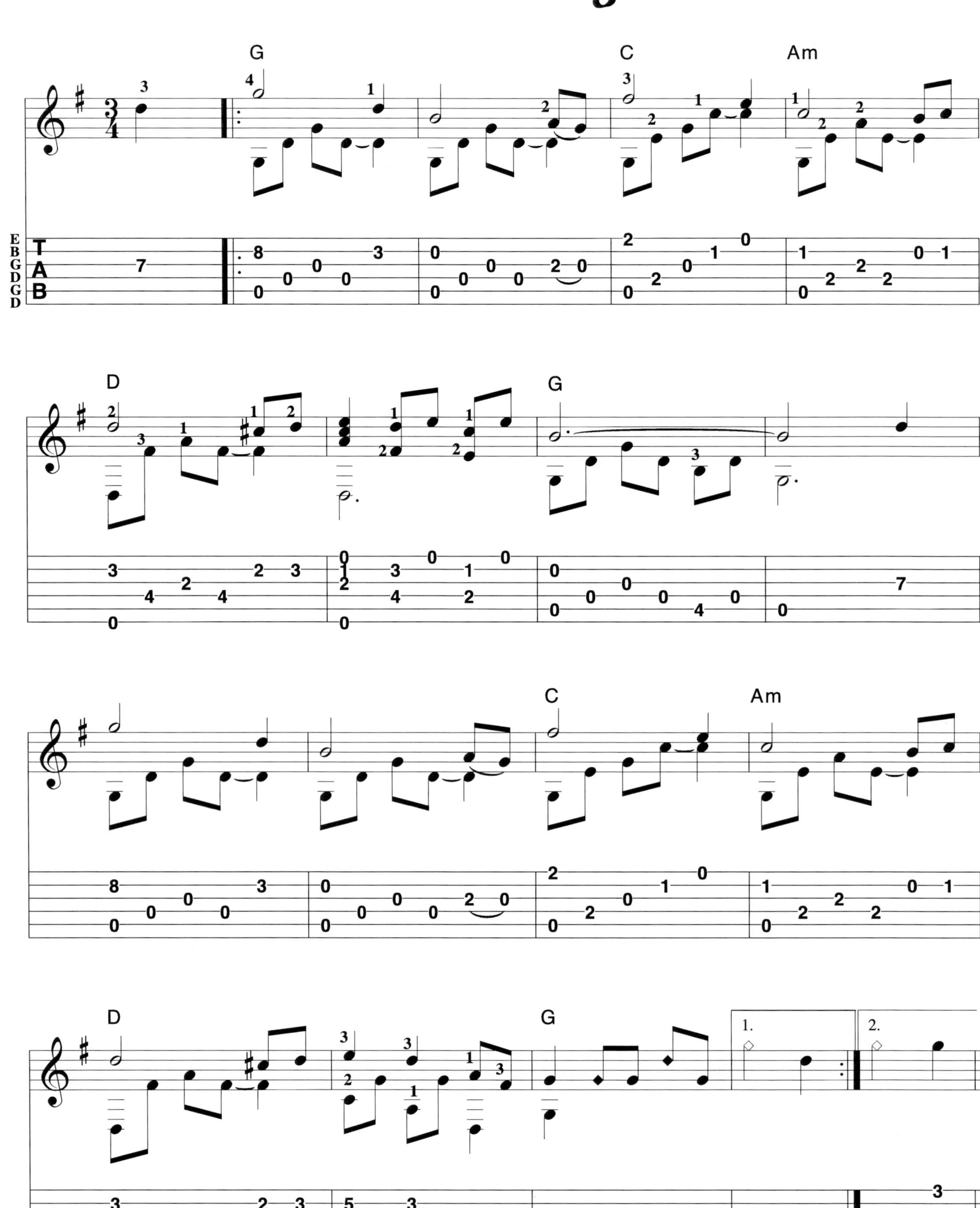

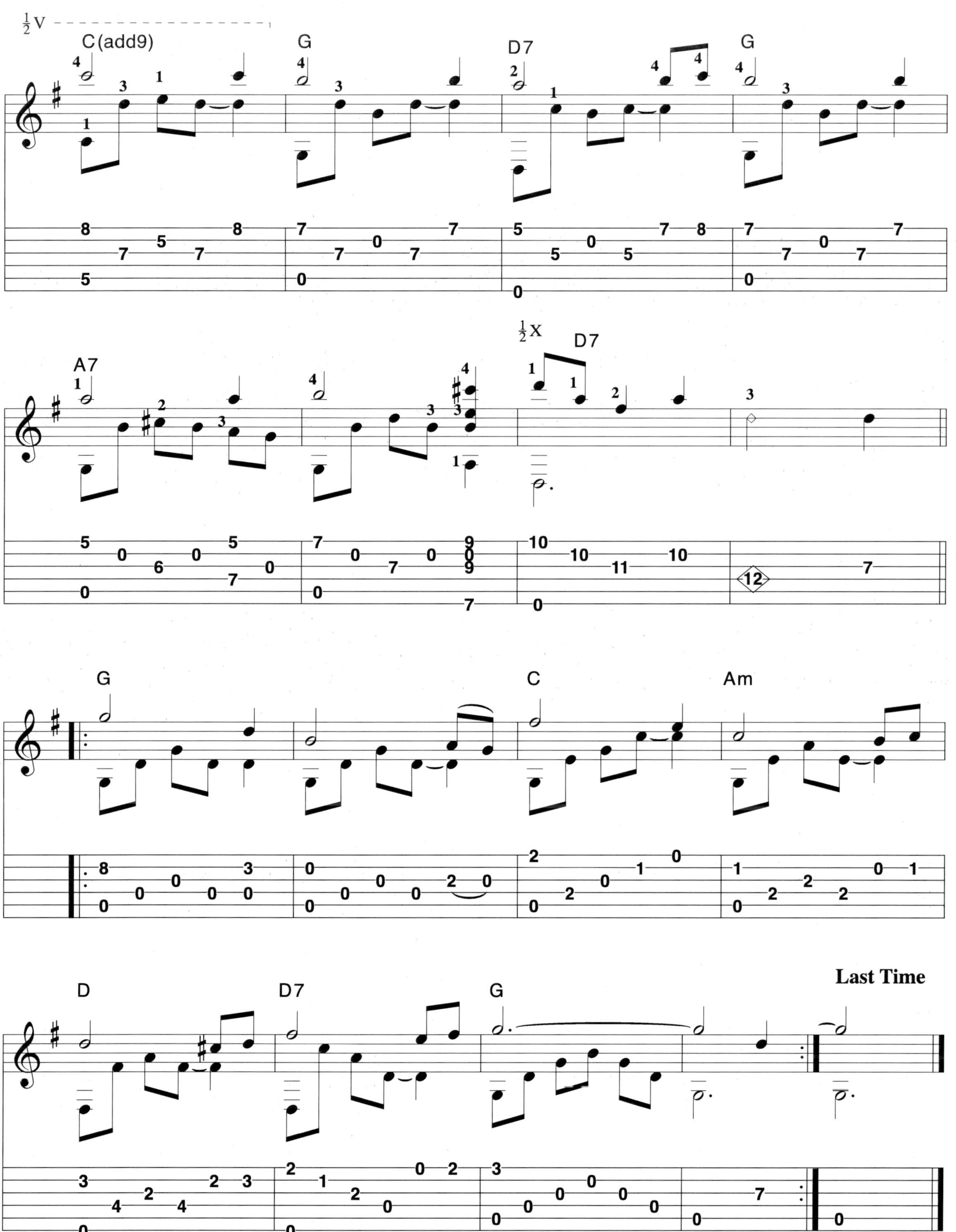
½V
C(add9)
G
D7
G
A7
½X
D7
G
C
Am
D
D7
G
Last Time
D.C.

# Chevy Chase

A very old tune and a favorite with pipers. The battle of Chevy Chase was fought in 1388 between the Douglas family and the Percy family over hunting rights in the Cheviot Hills. A chase was an area where hunting took place.

Technical Notes - Tune the guitar DGDGAD low to high.

Play the tune in a somber manner.

# Chevy Chase

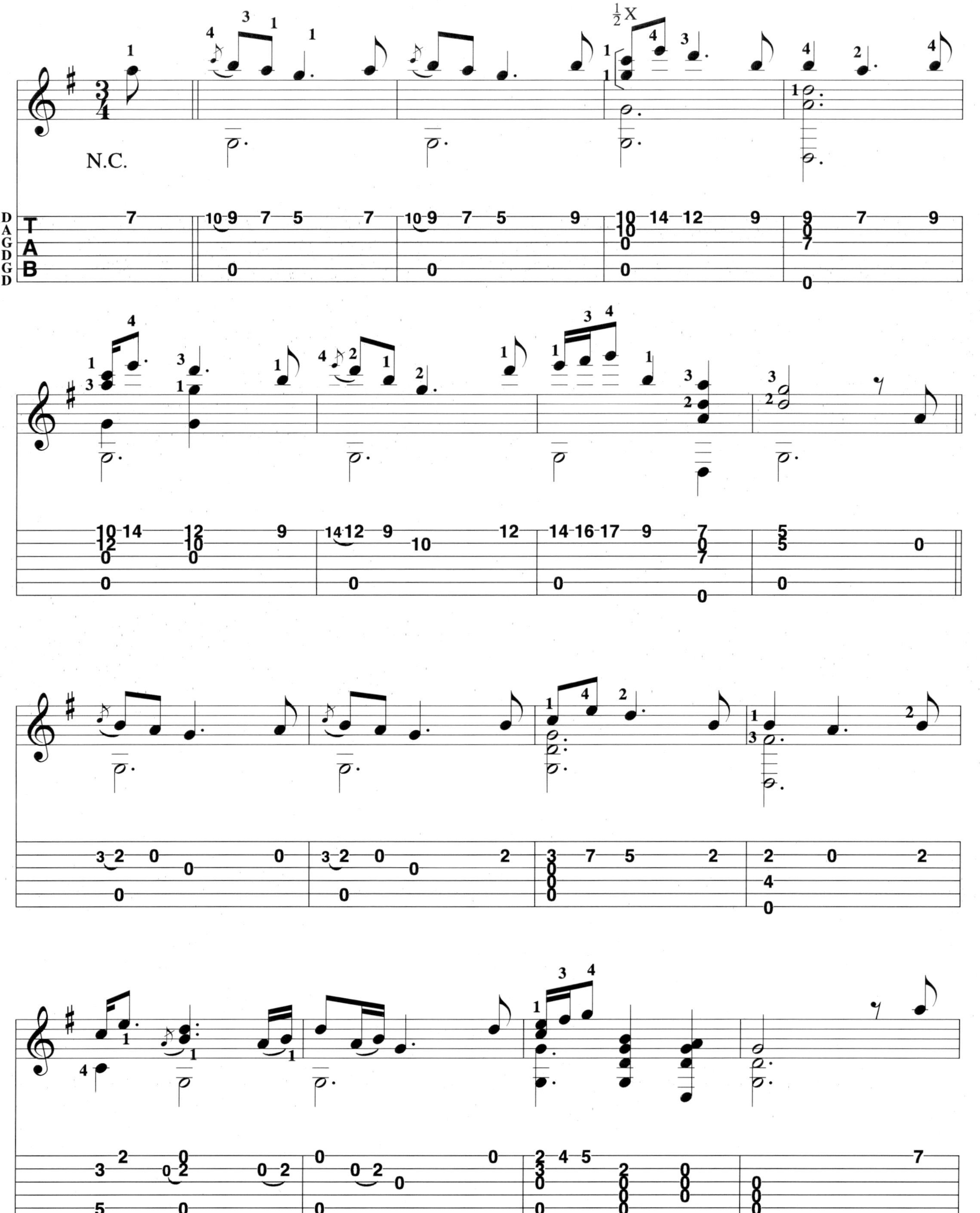

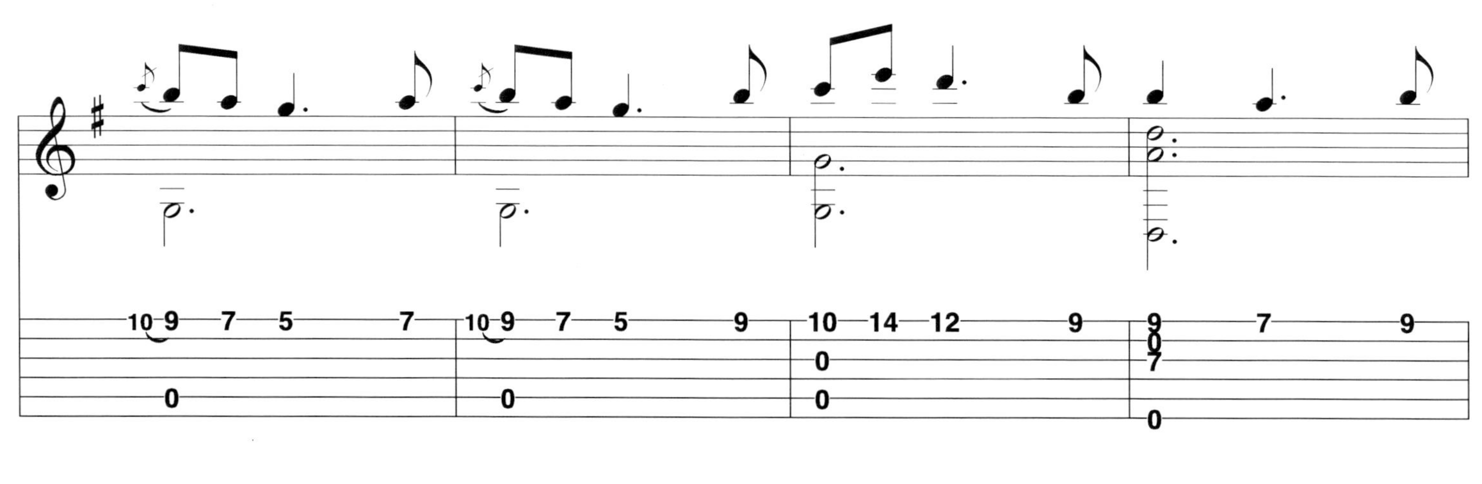

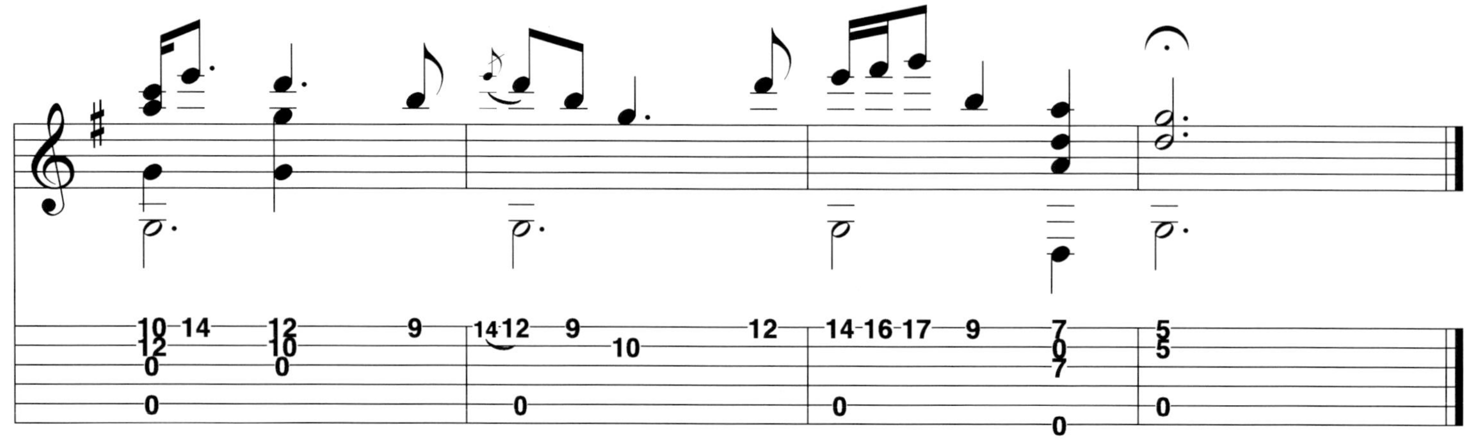

# Lea Riggs

This is a very nice little march and sounds quite Scottish.

Technical Notes - Tune the guitar DGDGBE low to high.

For this kind of cross-string tune the "right hand" fingering I use is as follows:

- 4th, 3rd, middle and index fingers for the 1st 2nd 3rd and 4th strings respectively.
- If you have another method then use it.

There is really nothing difficult about the left hand fingering. Just remember to let the strings ring by keeping the fingers on as long as possible.

# Lea Riggs

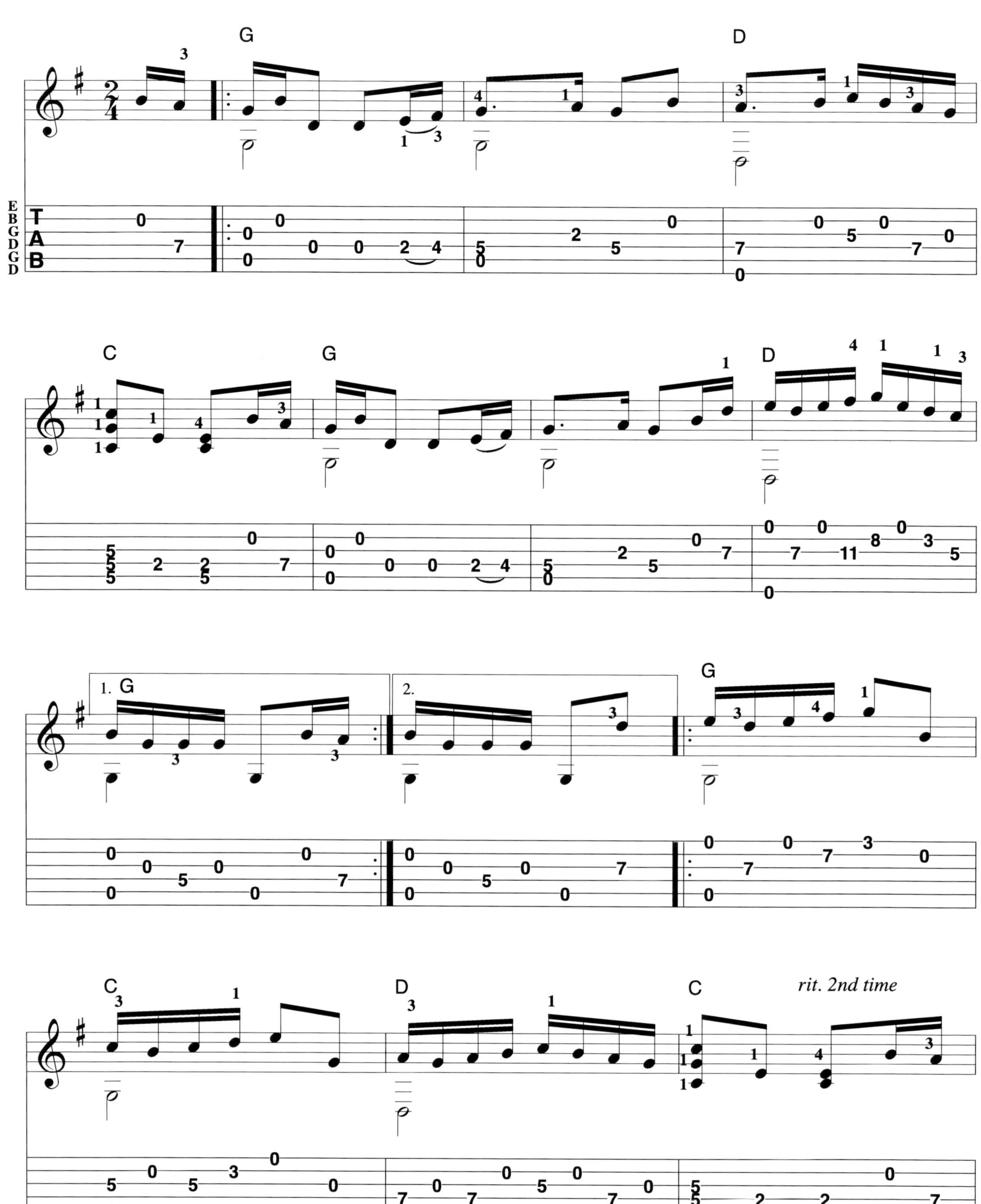

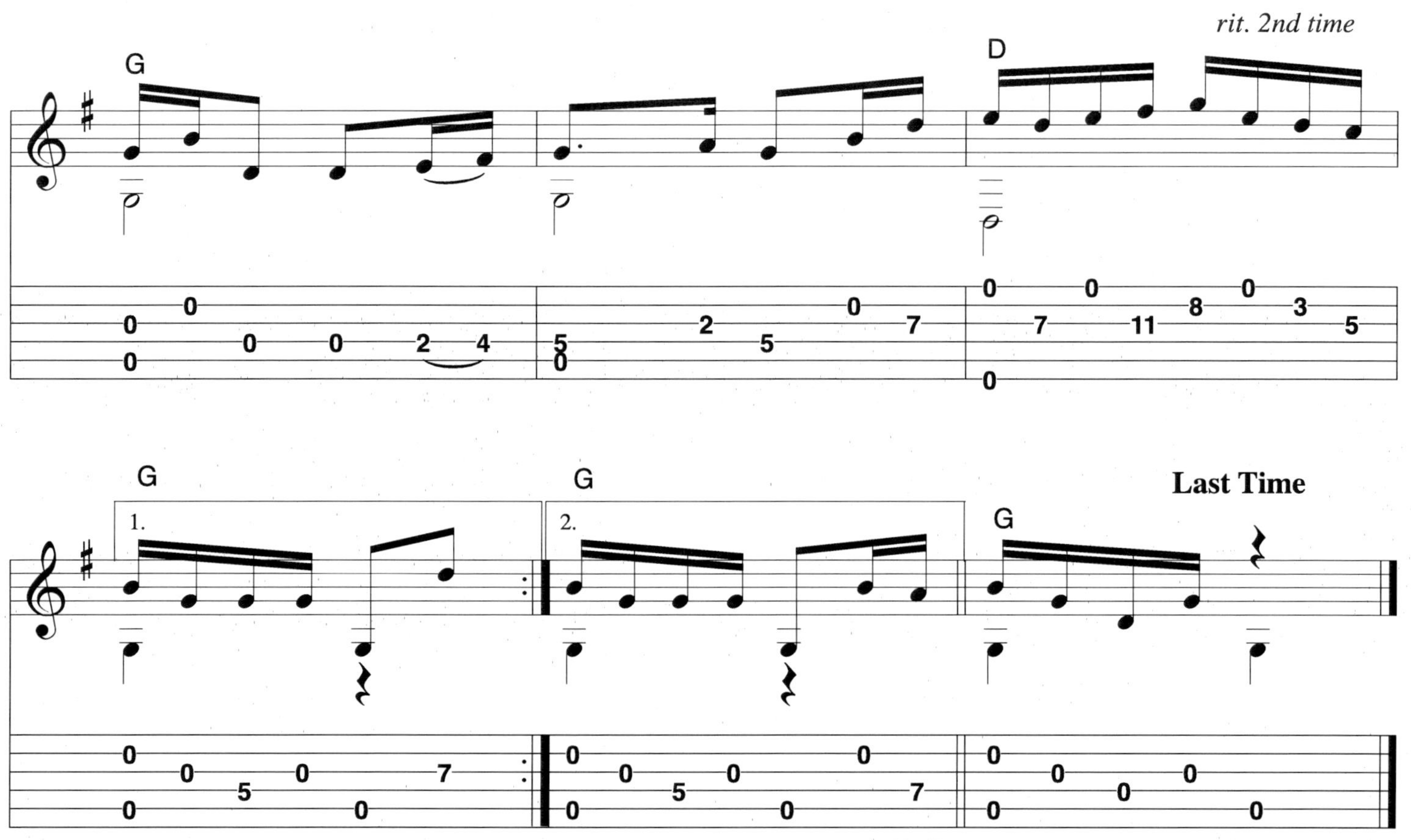
rit. 2nd time
G
D
G
1.
G
2.
Last Time
G
D.C.

# Noble Squire Dacre

This can be played as a slow march or a very slow air.

Technical Notes - Tune the guitar DGDGBE low to high.

The finger snaps are probably the most difficult thing about this tune. Practice them slowly and they will come.

# Noble Squire Dacre

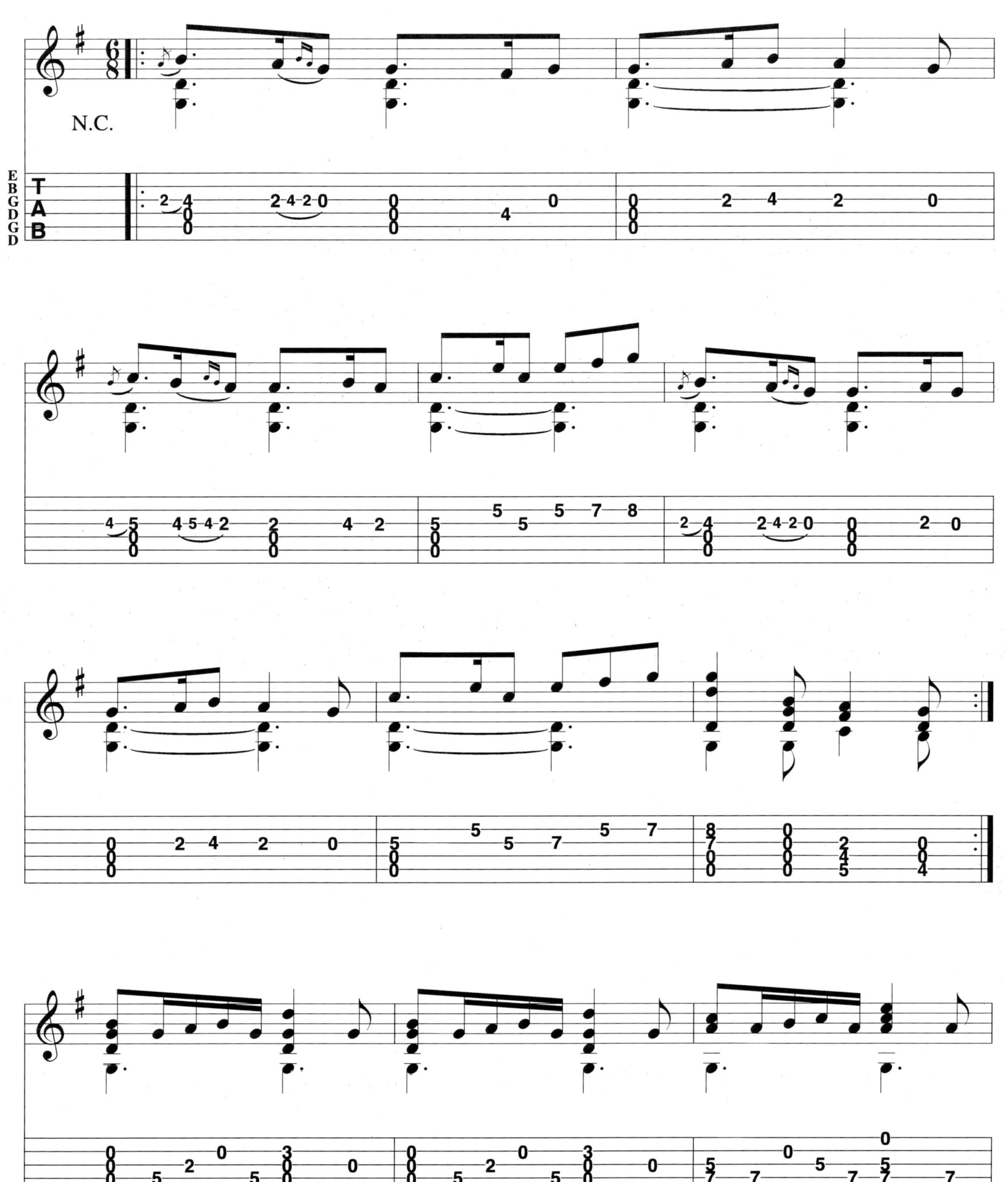

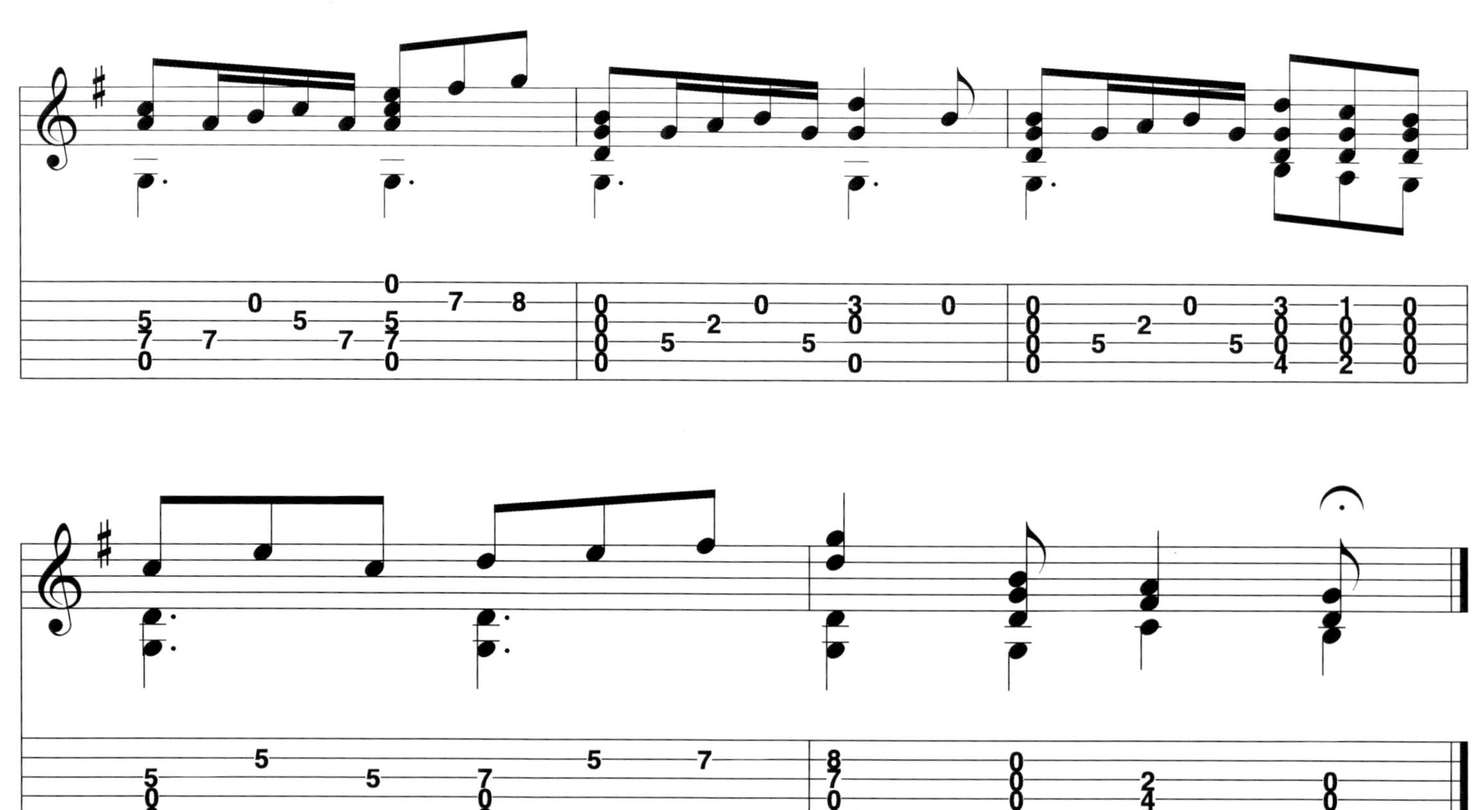

*D.C.*

# Dolía

## (Dolly-Ah)

A Newcastle street song that dates from the latter part of the 18th century.

Technical Notes - Tune the guitar in standard tuning.

There really is nothing difficult about this arrangement. Just keep the bass going and the marching style will come naturally.

# Dolía

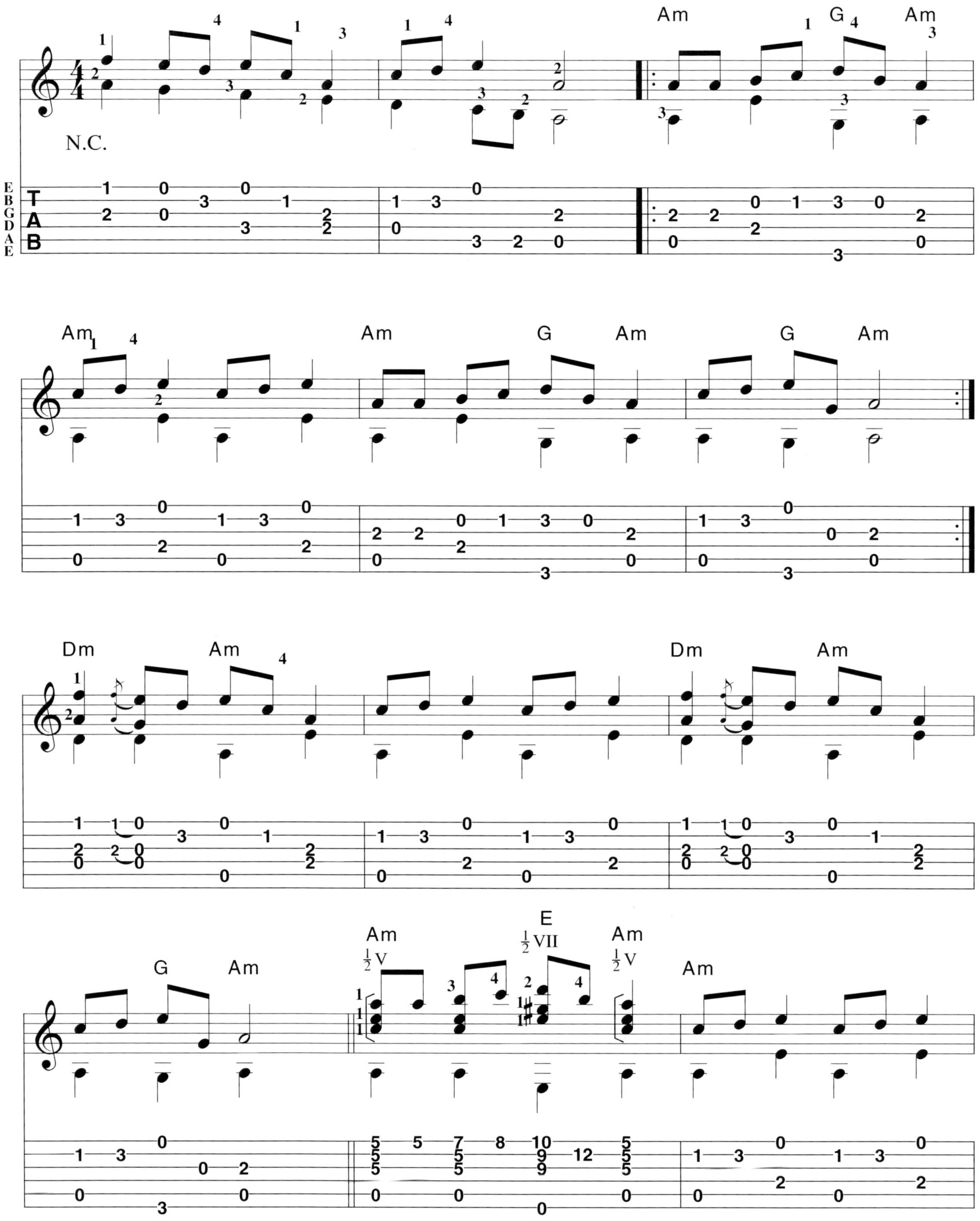

N.C.
Am G Am

Am Am G Am G Am

Dm Am Dm Am

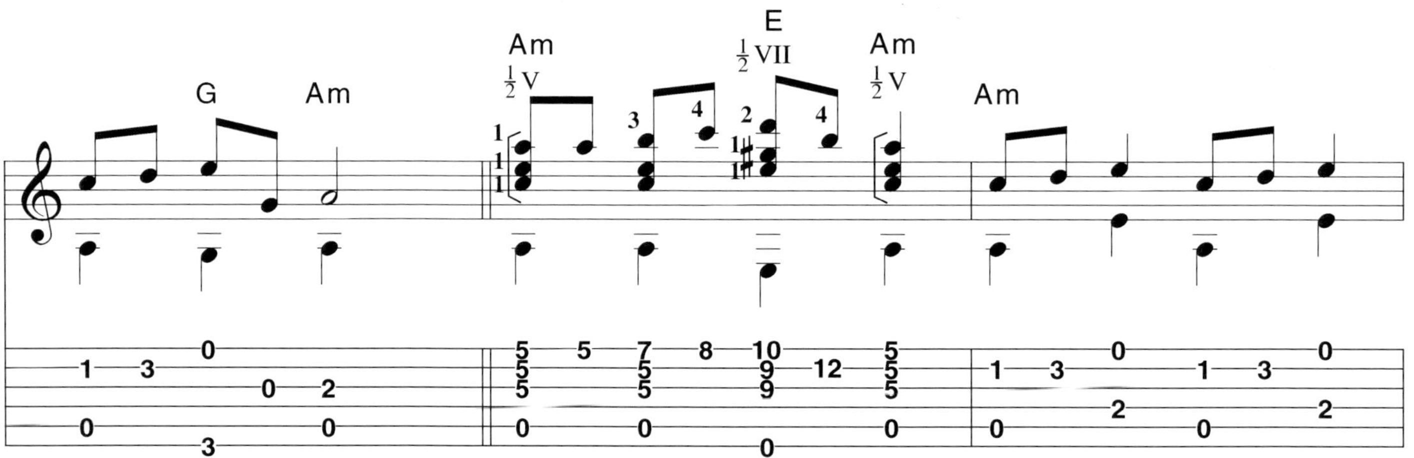

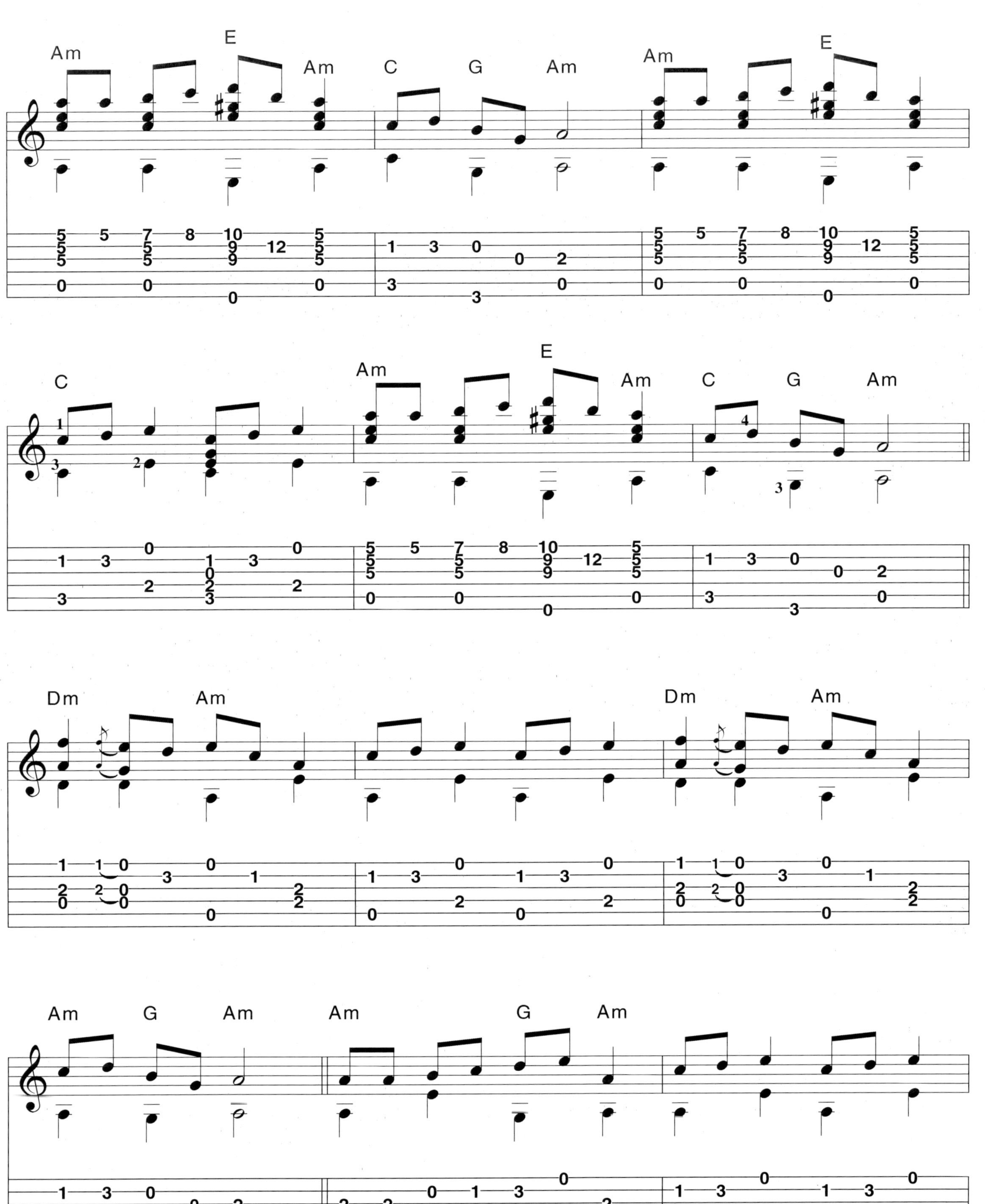
Am
E
Am
C
G
Am
Am
E
Am
C
Am
E
Am
C
G
Am
Dm
Am
Dm
Am
Am
G
Am
Am
G
Am

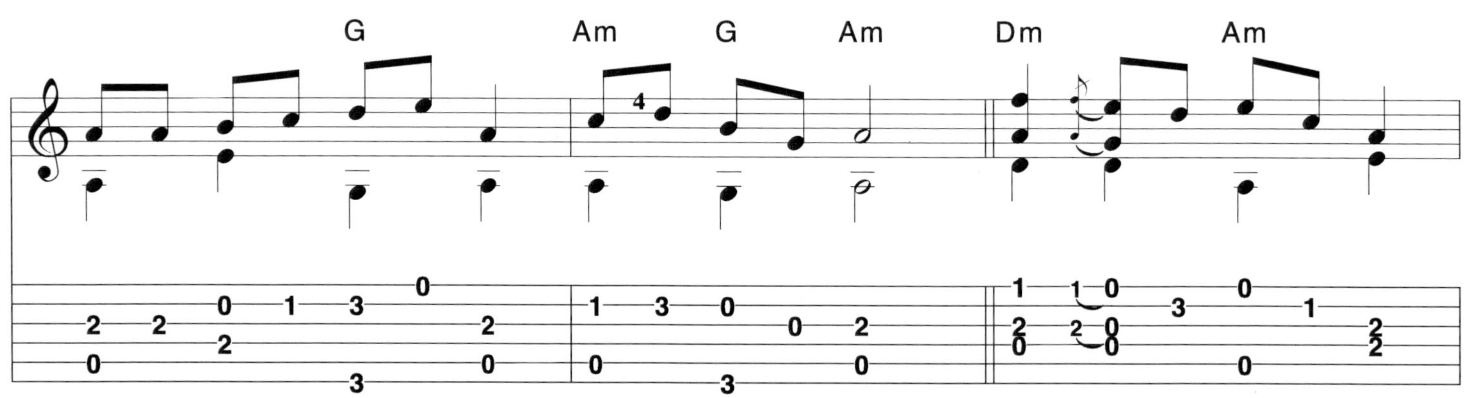
G
Am
G
Am
Dm
Am

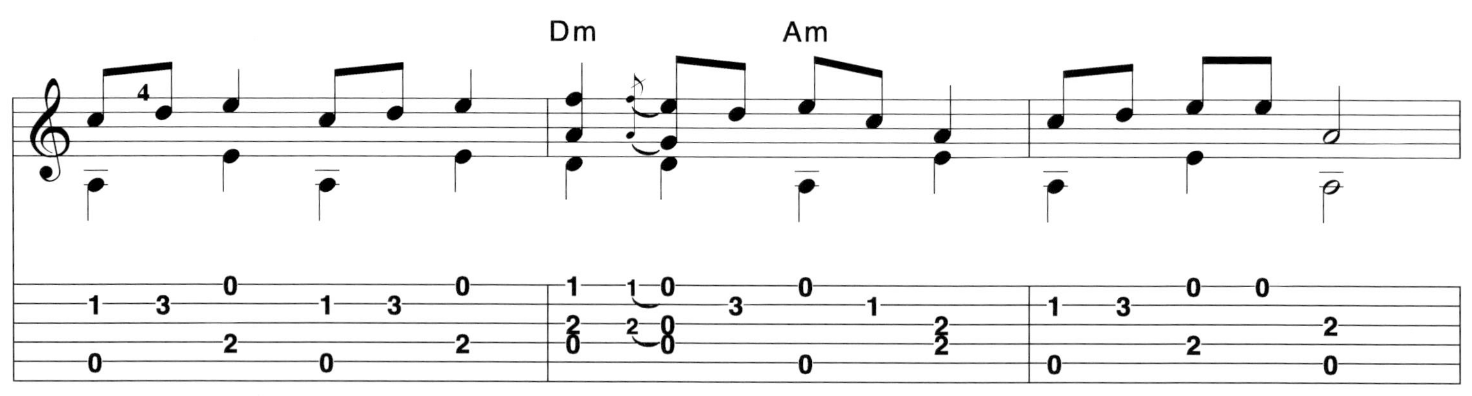
Dm
Am

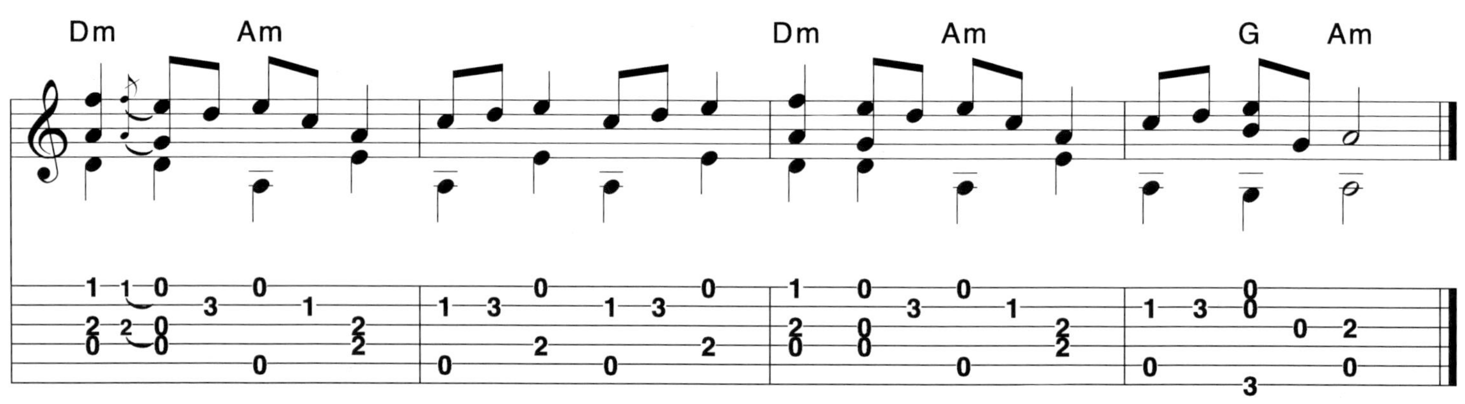
Dm
Am
Dm
Am
G
Am

# Are You My Hinny Burd

A 19th century Newcastle street song. Hinny is a term of endearment and burd is another name for a girl.

Technical Notes - Tune the guitar DADGBE low to high.

The change from the G chord to the A chord in bar 9 can be tricky. Take it slowly, if necessary practice the G chord separately.

# Are You My Hinny Burd

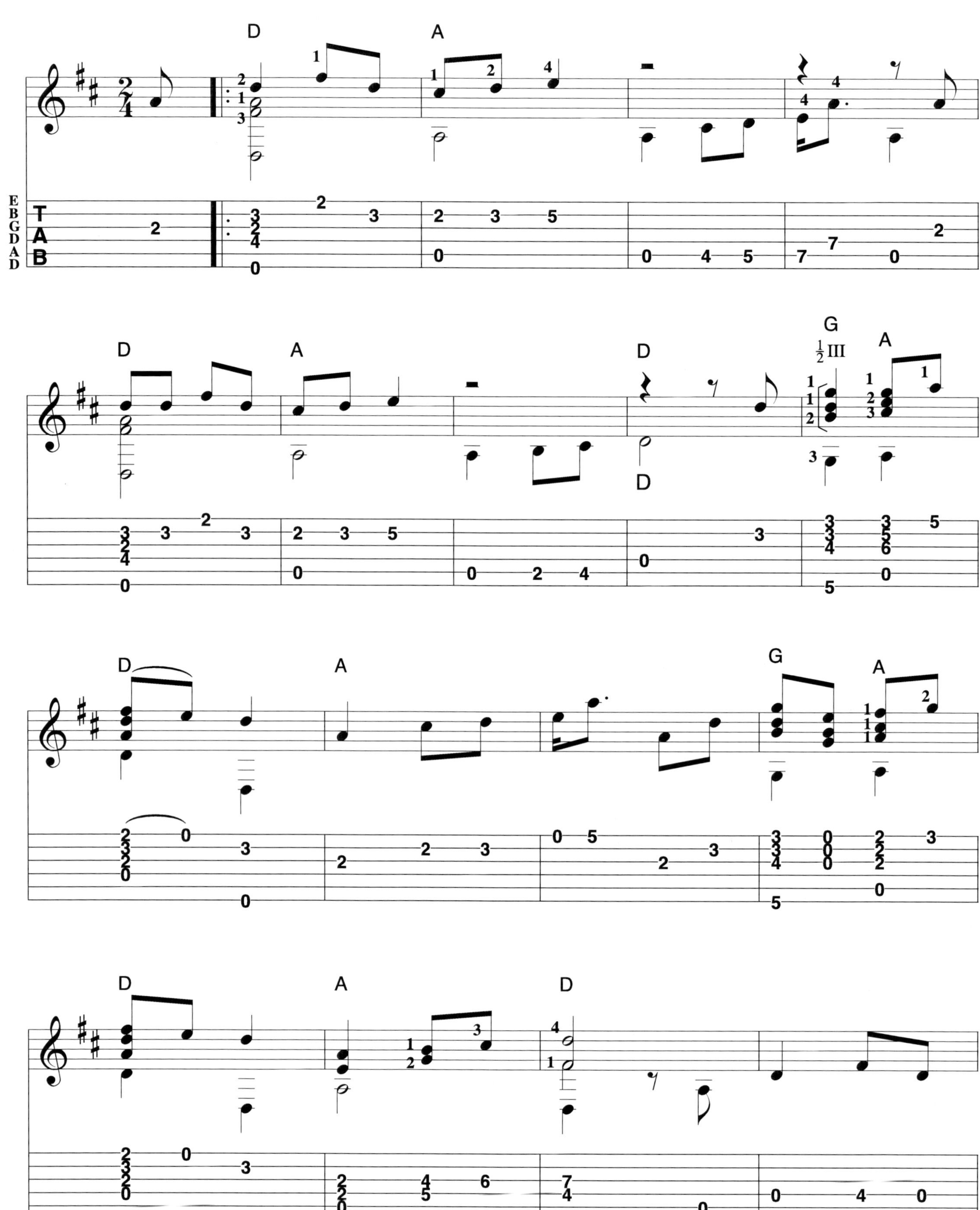

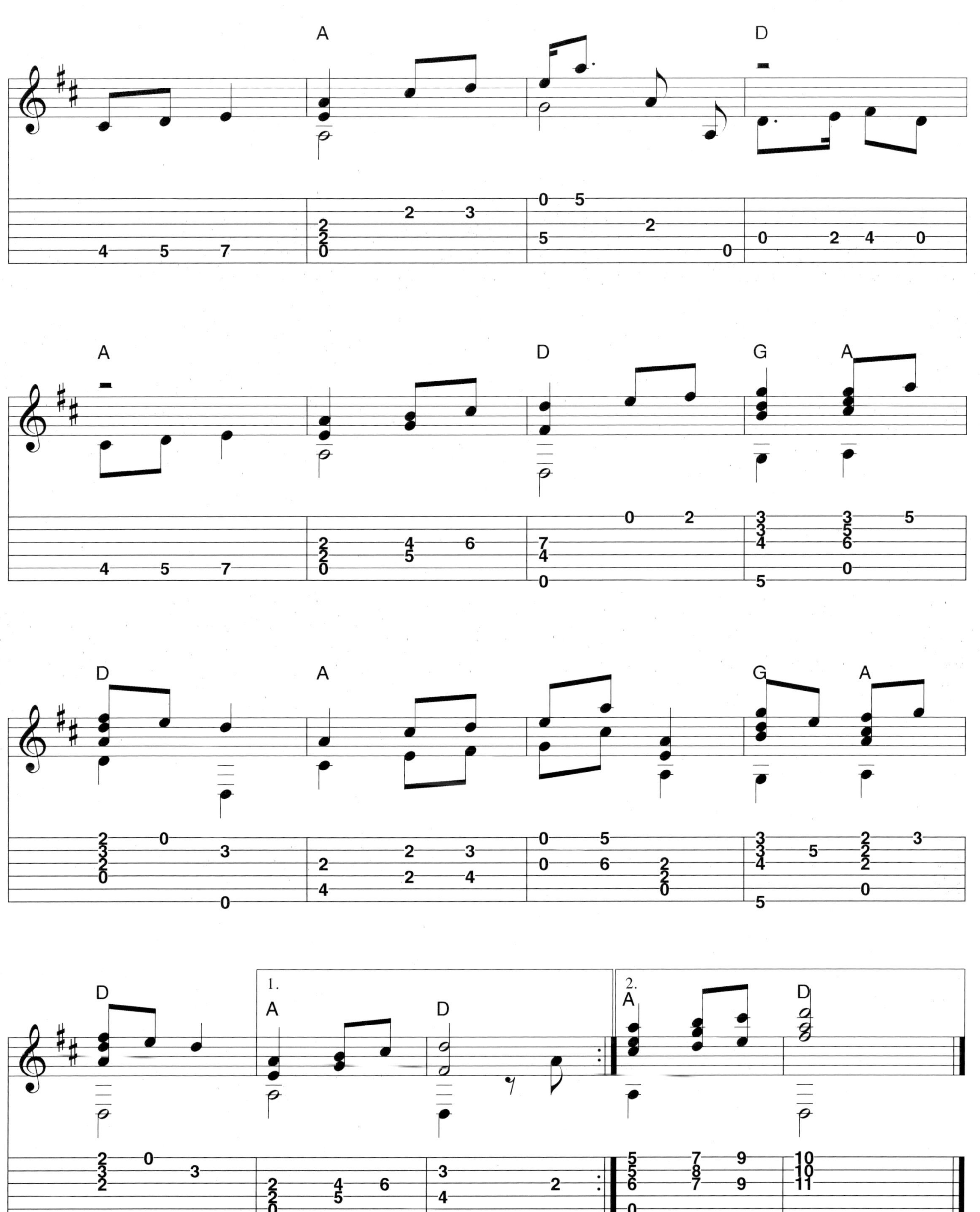
A
D
A
D
G
A
D
A
G
A
D
1.
A
D
2.
A
D

# The Breamish

The Breamish is a river in Northumberland.

Technical Notes - Tune the guitar DADGAD low to high.

This is quite a simple arrangement. Practice any stretches until they feel comfortable.

# The Breamish

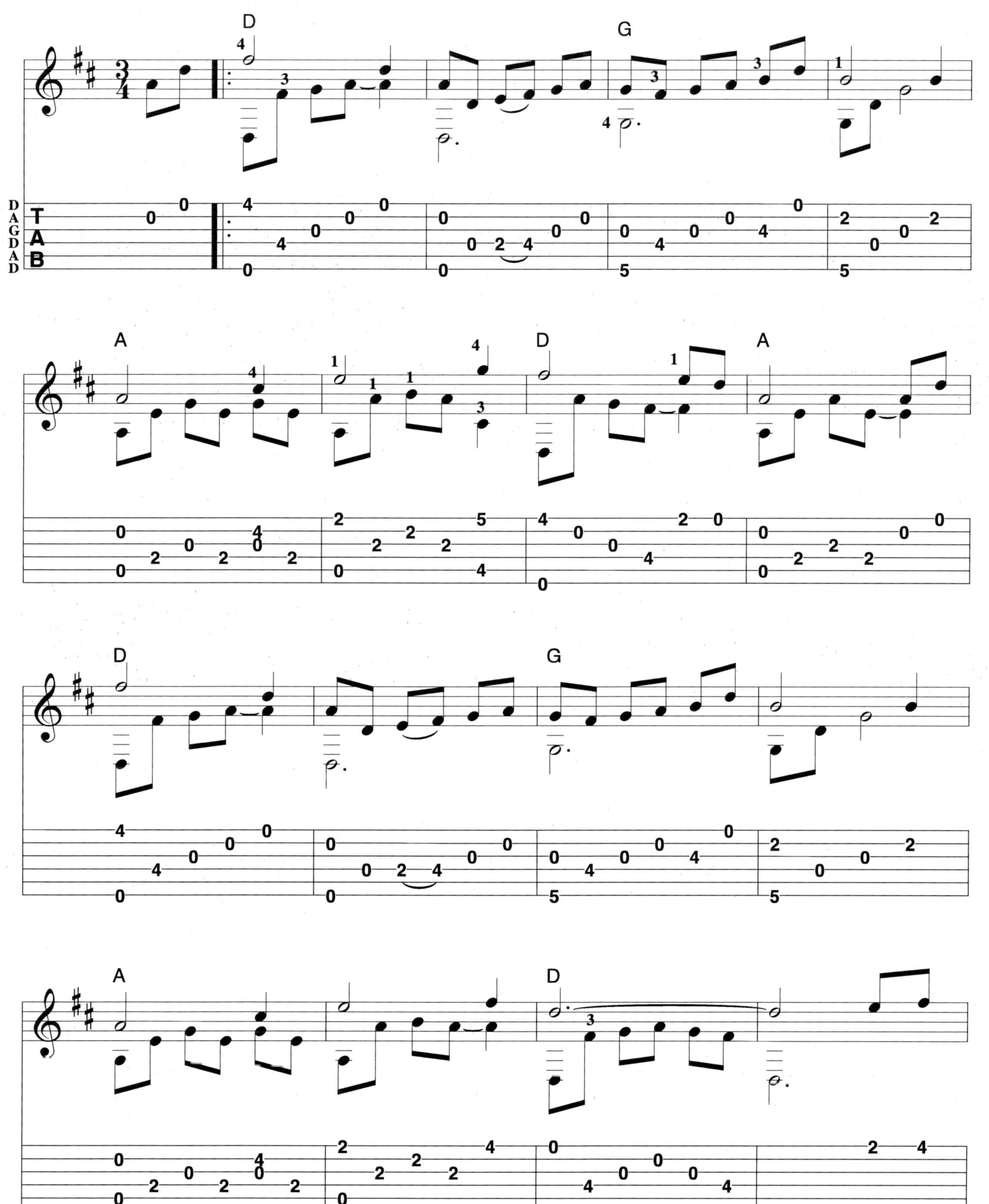

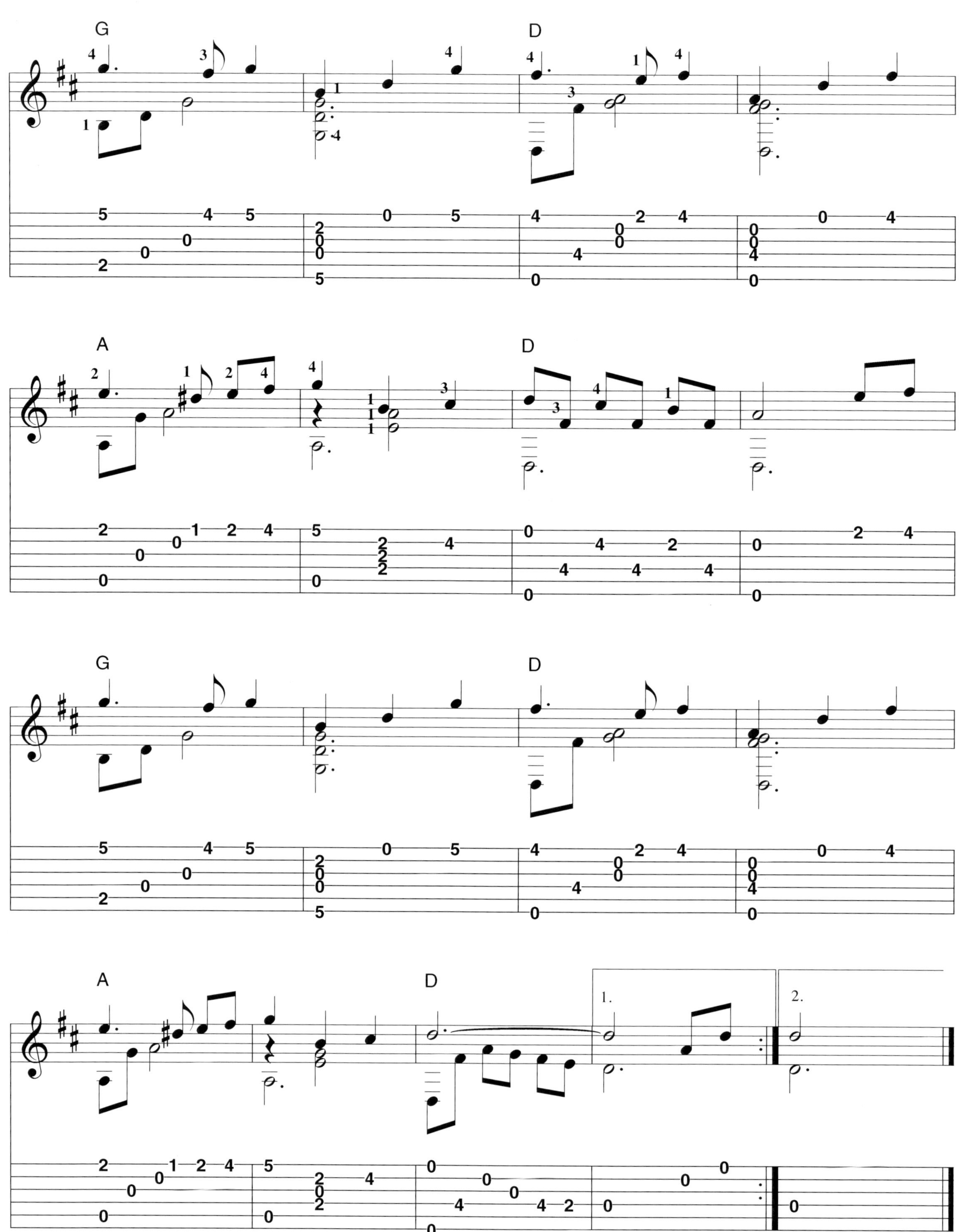
G
D
A
D
G
D
A
D
1.
2.

# Blow the Wind Southerly

A song with nautical connections. This version of the melody can be found in the Northumbrian Pipers Tune book.

Technical Notes - Tune the guitar DADGAD low to high.

Practice any stretches until they feel comfortable.

# Blow the Wind Southerly

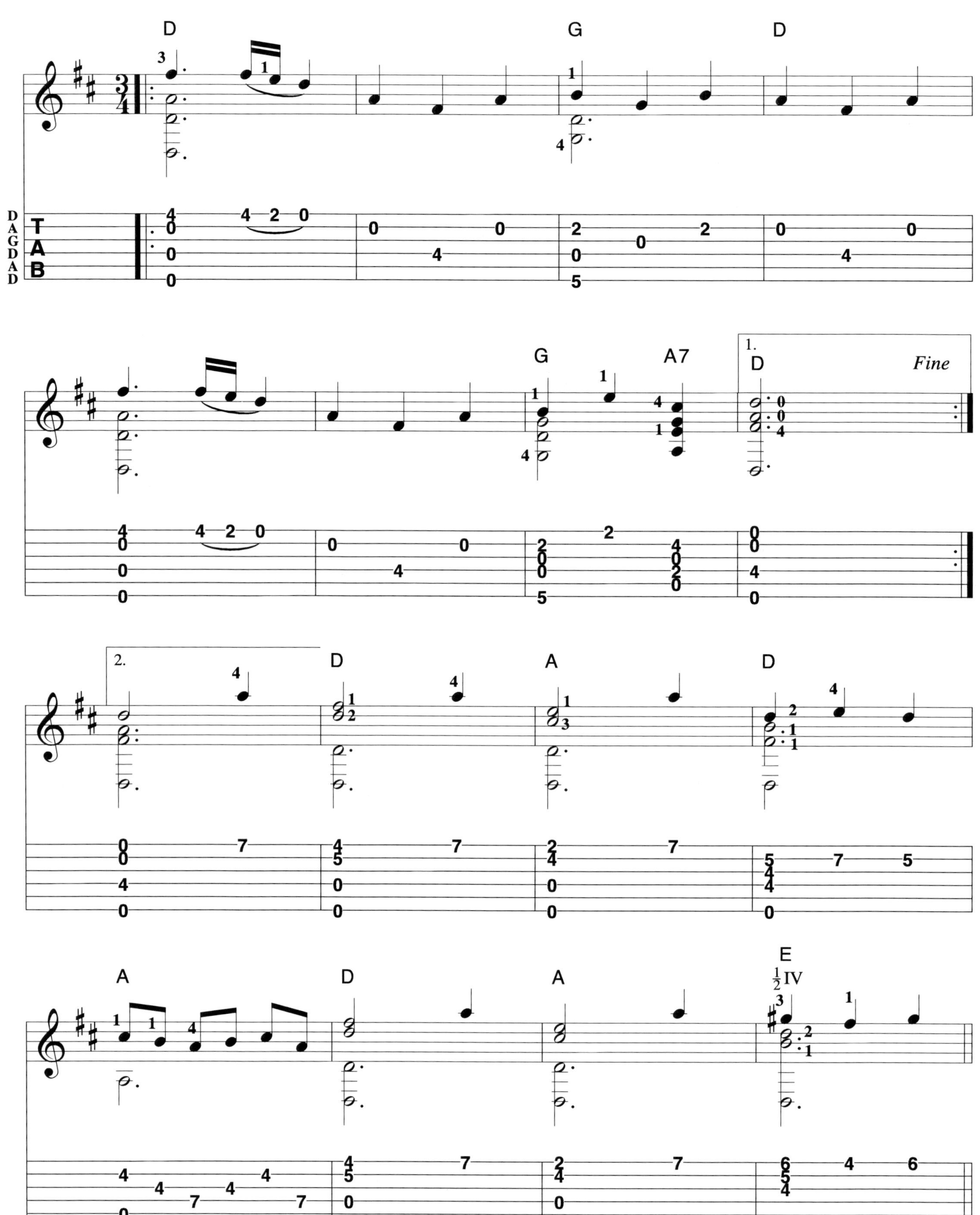

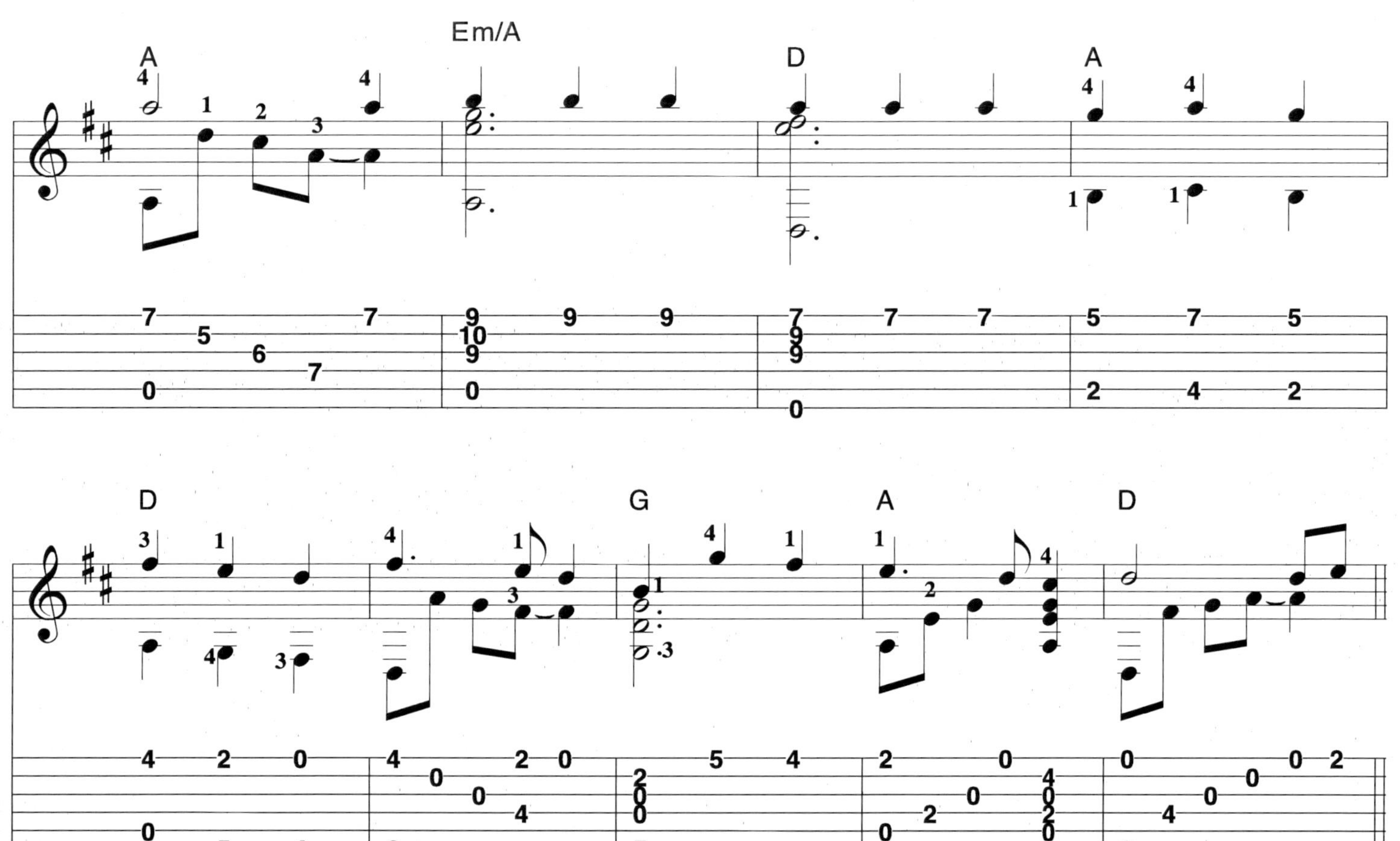


*D.C. al Fine*

# Here's the Tender Coming

Another nautical song. A beautiful, simple melody this one.

Technical Notes - Tune the guitar DADF♯AD low to high.

Mute the bass notes for the melody when you play it the 1st time through then let them ring the second time.

# Here's the Tender Coming

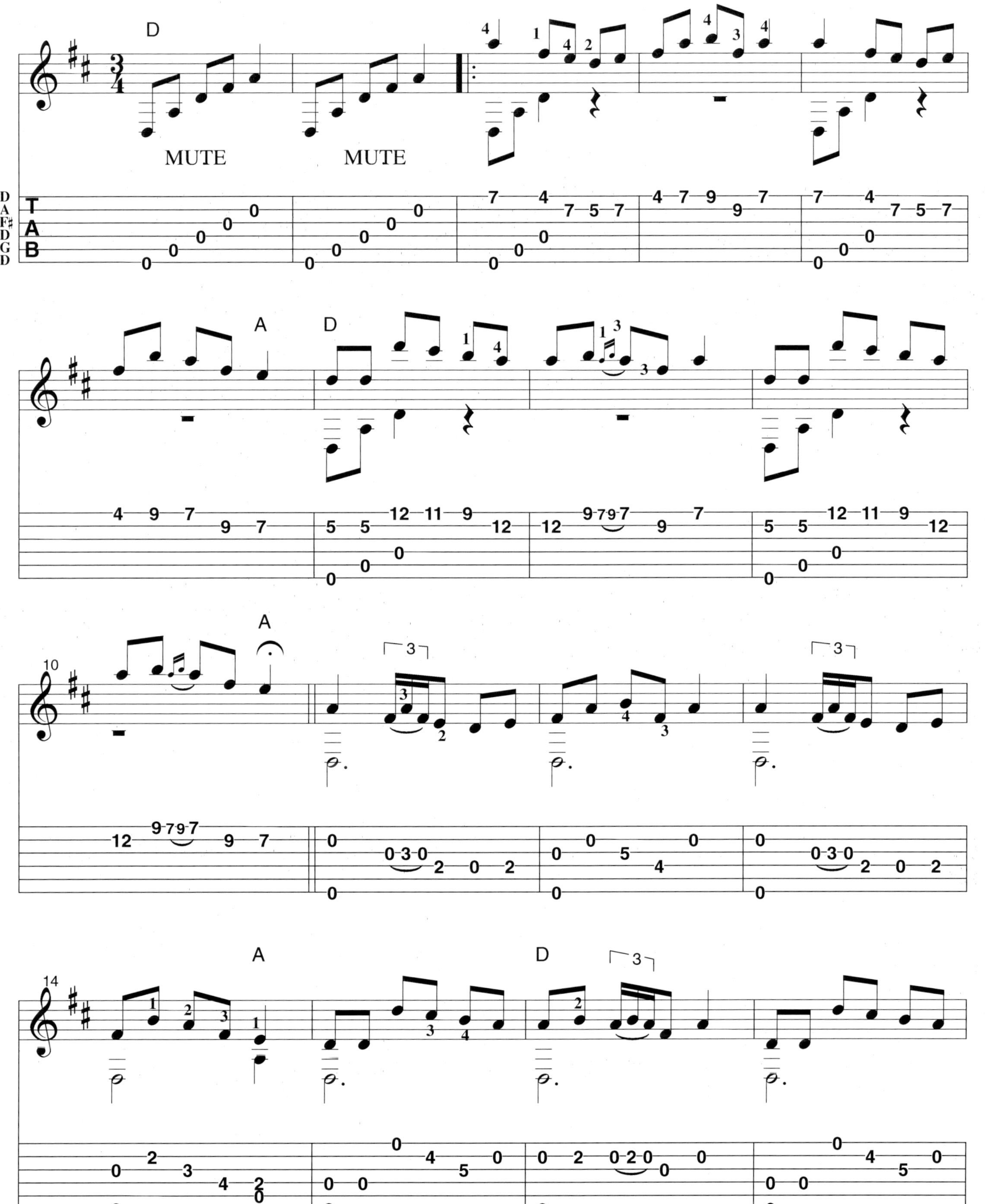

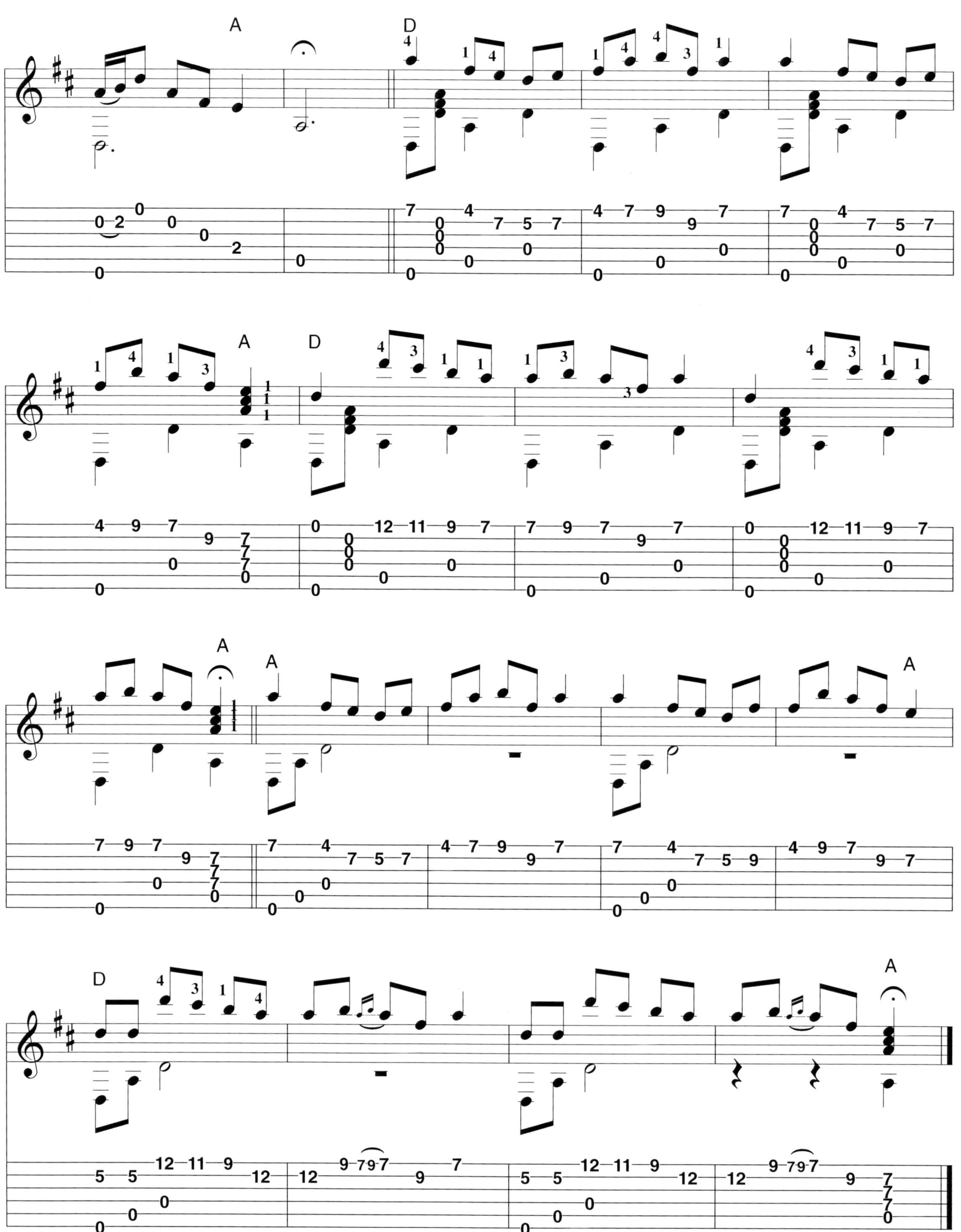
A
D
A
D
A
A
A
D
A

# Waters of Tyne

This is a much loved Northumbrian song.

Technical Notes - Tune the guitar DADGAD low to high.
In the middle, the melody shifts to the bass strings. Try to bring it out by using a slight vibrato.

# Waters of Tyne

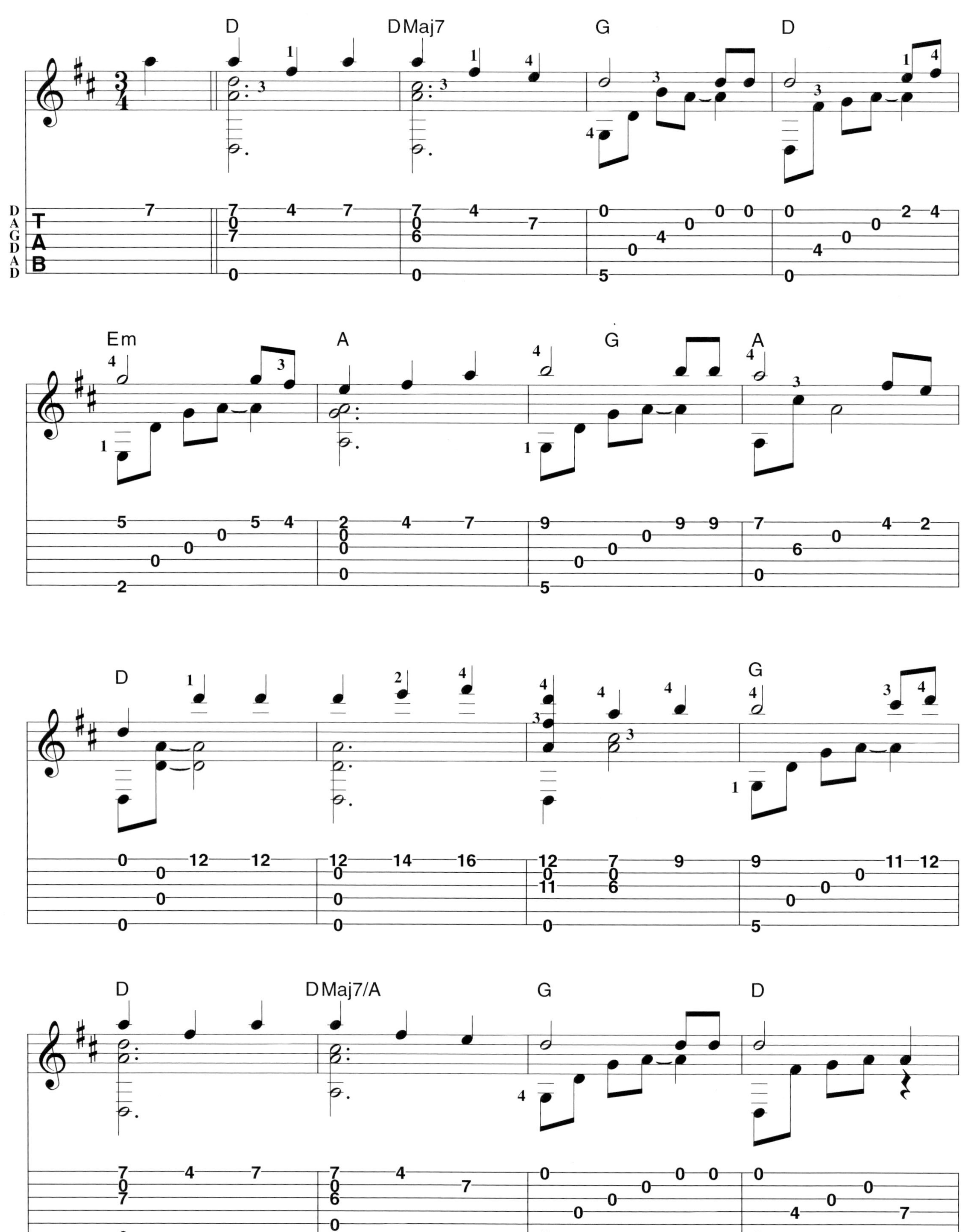

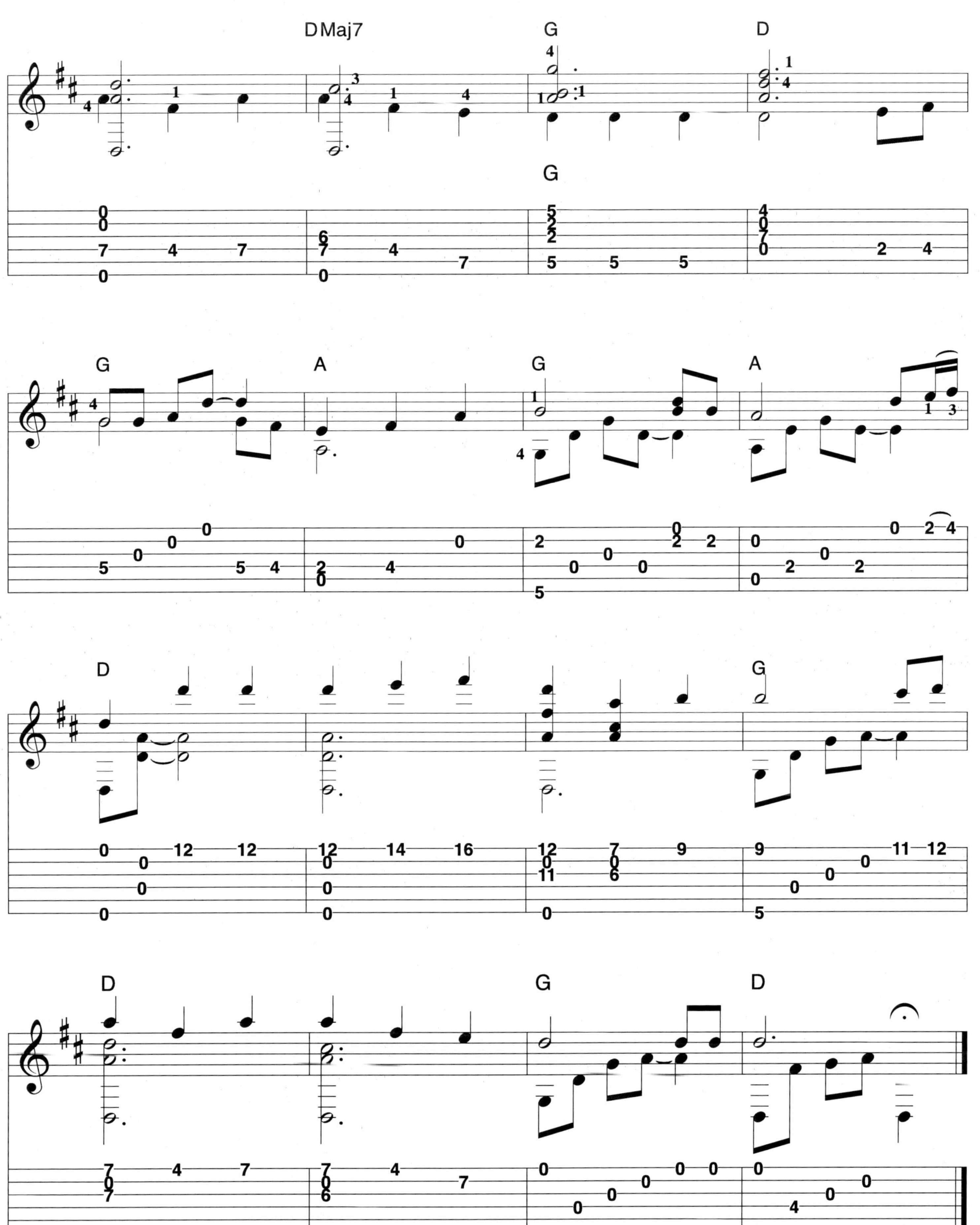
DMaj7
G
D
G
G
A
G
A
D
G
D
G
D

# Bill Brennan

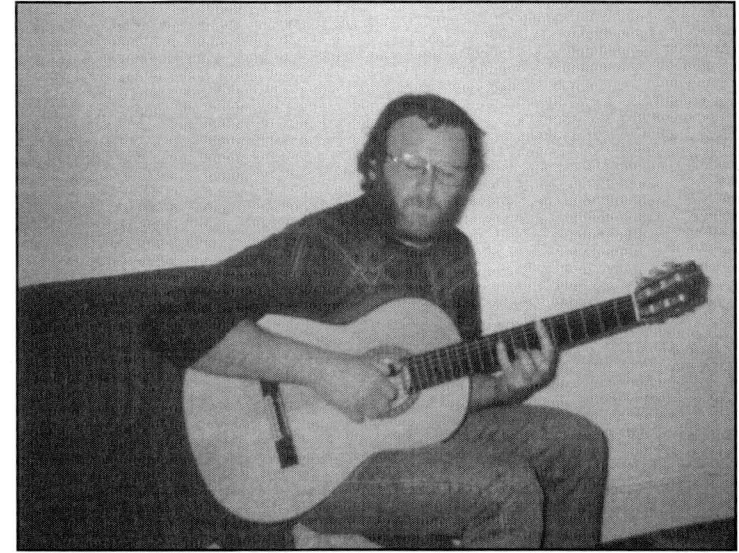

Bill Brennan is married with one daughter and lives in the North East of England. Bill has lived all his life in the town of Prudhoe, in the County of Northumberland.

He started playing guitar when he was 10 years of age, and has been a professional guitarist since 1970.

In the sixties, he played in local rock/pop bands, folk clubs, and jazz ensembles. In the years since then, he has played in various musical productions, and has performed solo jazz, classical, blues and traditional guitar.

He has been a guitar teacher since the late sixties and he now teaches at local schools, colleges and the University of Northumbria in Newcastle upon Tyne.

*Irish and Scottish Airs and Ballads for Acoustic Guitar*, Irish and *Scottish Airs and Ballads for Fingerstyle Guitar*, and *Irish, Scottish and Border Melodies for Flatpicking Guitar* was published by Mel Bay Publications.

By tapping the rich vein of local folk music, and adapting it for his books, Bill has combined his passion for guitar, with his deep appreciation of the traditional music of Ireland, Scotland and his own Border country.

– Yvonne Brennan

# Additional Celtic Guitar Titles
# *available through*
# Mel Bay Publications, Inc.

| | | |
|---|---|---|
| 99248M | Easy Celtic Solos for Fingerstyle Guitar | Book/audio set |
| 98435 | Irish Folk Songs for Classical Guitar | Book |
| 98147 | Jigs and Reels for Classic Guitar | Book |
| 98282 | Steve Kaufman's Encyclopedia of Celtic Tunes for Flatpicking Guitar | Book |
| 99805BCD | Celtic Melodies for Fingerpicking Guitar | Book/audio set |
| 99357 | Scottish Traditional Music for Guitar: in DADGAD and Open G Tunings | Book |

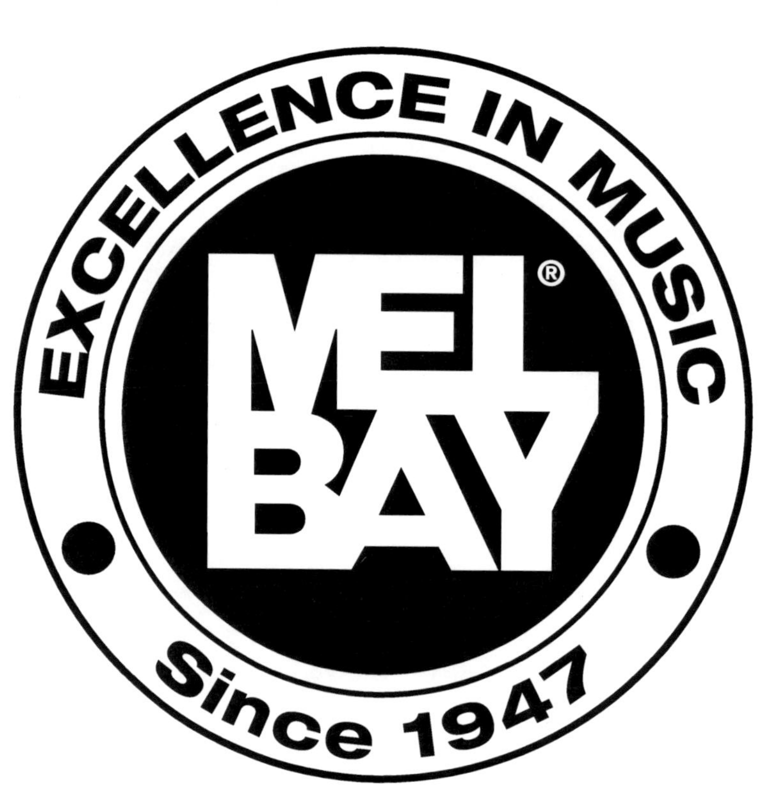
EXCELLENCE IN MUSIC
MEL BAY®
Since 1947